ARRIVAL PRESS

POETIC ART

Edited

By

TIM SHARP

First published in Great Britain in 1997 by
ARRIVAL PRESS
1 - 2 Wainman Road, Woodston,
Peterborough, PE2 7BU

All Rights Reserved

Copyright Contributors 1996

HB ISBN 1 85786 531 6
SB ISBN 1 85786 526 X

Foreword

The Arts are an important part of self-expression within individuals. Poetry is one of them.

This fine compilation of verse has inspired poets who have a passion for music, dance and painting, to mention but a few.

This has given poets from all walks of life a chance to show their appreciation towards *The Arts* by the use of expression, in poetry.

This book is a delightful read, I hope you enjoy it as much as I did whilst editing it.

Tim Sharp
Editor

CONTENTS

Talent Trove	Ruth Daviat	1
Natural Art	Dorothy Johnstone	2
Impressions of The Impressionists	Barbara Fosh	3
The Dancing Years	Reg Morris	4
Cool Thinking	M C Wood	5
One Of The Arts	Jean Hendrie	6
The Onlooker's Delight	R Medland	7
Harriet	Osamah Gahin	8
Hidden Depths	Susan Mullinger	9
Work Of Art	J Facchini	10
Poetic Art	R Duck	11
Time To Dream	Bell Ferris	12
Middle Age	H Cullum	13
Untitled	Shaun Hopkins	14
The Artist's Tale	Rose Worms	15
Ballet Shoes	Joan Hands	16
Appreciate	T Read	17
Artistic Trails	Danny Pyle	18
Bon Giorno - Madam Butterfly	Paul Gold	19
A Study On Prose	Kevin J Foulger	20
Art Is For Me	Jeanette Gaffney	21
A Bundle Of Joy	Lucy Green	22
Poet	J Stephens	23
Artistic Endeavour	Kenneth McPhee	24
Dance	M Cook	25
Waiting . . .	Gig	26
The River Dance	Marie Barker	27
Cloister Conspiracy	Grace Wade	28
Bio-Poem	Perry McDaid	29
I Go To Them To Find Their Souls	Claire-Lyse Sylvester	30
Art's Most Princely Shrine	Thomas W Split	31
Strategy	Monica R Rehill	32
My Dying Swan	Felicity Webster	33
Cake Capers	Marion Elizabeth Sherwood	34

The Masters	Glennis Horne	35
The Arts In Nature	Jenny Brownjohn	36
The Forgotten Manuscript	Anne Christabel Davey-Young	37
Cardiacs Best Band In The World	Stephen Adams	38
Dedicationn Of A Ballerina	Kathrine Summers	39
Swan Lake	Margaret Curzon-Howe	40
Hasland Theatre Company's 50th Anniversary: 1946-1996	Doreen Wheeldon	41
Creative Art	Pat Mear	42
Art	Simon Peterson	43
Arts And Crafts	Jean M White	44
Link	D L Redman	45
Maybe One Day . . .	Dennis Turner	46
Day Dreamer	Roy Hunter	48
Tap Dancing	Kerry Louise Hayley	49
Could It Be . . .?	Stan Morton	50
Art Or Commerce	Malcolm Brown	51
Work Of Art	Nicola Regan	52
Art V Science	J Margaret Service	53
Master Class	Ann G Wallace	54
Thoughts	Brian George Wellsbury	55
The Modern Anthology	Gwynn Watt	56
The School's Household Musicians	Gillian Fisher	57
The Picture	Mary Buckingham	58
Classified	Emma Grainger	59
Pub Talk	Matthew Walmsley	60
Mall	Kevin Henderson	62
Art And Galleries	William FitzHugh	63
Metamorphosis!	Robert Denham	64
Writer's Urge	Mariella Cassar	65
Cup Of Tea	Steve Taylor	66
The Arts	Natasha Ward	67
Visual Arts	Donald Burt	68
Dear Poet Laureate	Afur Mo	69
Little Ballerina	Irene Carter	70
The Kiss	Marian Reid	71

An English Artist	G A Burgess	72
Creative Art, I Love You	Kenneth Mood	73
Art Gallery	Eleanor Nesbitt	74
Writer	Les Merton	75
Sawbridgeworth Musical Youth Theatre	Lynsey Bessent	76
Spice Of Life	Trevor Barnes	77
Dancing	Verity Denton	78
No Overture	Mary Spain	79
Ambition	Freda Tester-Ellis	80
The Dance From The Past	Valerie Sutton	81
Actors	Gladys Gayler	82
The Master Artist	Michael Morris	83
Of Life And Art	Kathleen Scatchard	84
Emily Hatch	Brenda Allen	85
Words	Tania Varndell	86
The Dancer	Carolyn Finch	87
Ballet	David Bennett	88
My Picture	R P Scannell	89
The Skaters	Joan Heybourn	90
The Art Of Creating	Anne Black	91
All In The Name Of . . . Art	J M Hefti-Whitney	92
Poet	John Bracken	93
Compromise	Doris Holland	94
Symphony Number Seven	Alan Swift	95
More Than One String To The Bow	R E Ward	96
The Artist Within	W Curran	97
I Wanted To Keep You	J A Lawrence	98
Sir John	Lydia E Stanton	99
Tears Rained Down	Evelyn Sharman	100
Nature's Art Gallery	Ann-Marie Wall	101
I Don't Care What People Say	Fiona Stimpson	102
I Want You To Find Yourself	Ciaran Berry	103
Midtown Moondance	Alexander Shand Hudson	104
Sunflower	Marie Nieuwoudt	105

Lisa	P J Littlefield	106
The Swan	Bruce Ward	107
Poets On Poetry	Emma Kemm	108
First Impressions	Michael Gardner	109
Travelling In Imagination Through Arts	Marjorie Cowan	110
An Extract From Torvill And Dean - The Epic 'Bolero'	Linnet-Joy Allison	111
First Night	Dora Watkins	112
Two Left Feet	Brigid O'Donnell	113
Riverdance	Elizabeth Loy	114
Oh!	Mary Todd	115
A Question Of Art	Ray Dite	116
Words	Joan Vicente	117
Art And Joy	Anita M Slattery	118
The Destiny	Durlabh Singh	119
The Arts	Chris Ann Kent	120
What Do 'The Arts' Mean To You?	Maggie Goren	121
Our Damien And Others	John Spiby	122
Untitled	Joel Hammond	123
Anxious Sloth	Mary Gill	124
From My Experience	Wendy Sullivan	125
Untitled	Heather Muddiman	126
Artful Ways	Joyce Hockley	127
In The Good Room	Mary Devlin	128
The Canon Of Art	Lyn Mowat	129
The Masterpiece	Paul Frank Lewthwaite	130
Motivaton Blockage	Graham Hyde	131
Art In Nature	Roy Blackman	132
The Carousel	Michael Lyons	133
Self Expression	E R Gemmell	134
My Art	Josephine Miles	135
The Arts	Char March	136
The World Of The Arts	Aodhan McCardle	137
The Arts Can Be Everything	Andrew Tatham	138
Questions of Audience, Ownership and Intention	James M Nash	139

Expressions Of Passion	Anita Watts	140
Is There An Art In It?	Anthony Gibson	141
Painting A Creation	Alastair Buchanan	142
Acting	E Smith	143
A Landscape Of Water Colour, Pastels And 2HB	James S Jarvis	144
Specially Commissioned	Paddy Douglas	145
Tribute To Pam Ayres	Geoff Tullett	146
Monet's Gift	Bettina Jones	147
Art Form	Fred Tighe	148
The Picture	Joyce M Turner	149
Cornelius Crud	Brenda Soderberg	150
A Poet	Sheila Waller	151
Music Lessons	John Kelly	152
Opening Night	C Clarke	153
Modern Art	Julie Ashpool	154
Essential Drama	Alasdair Aston	155

TALENT TROVE

The populace, souls I may have snubbed, ignored,
Had never really left, departure made,
For, out of nowhere, a paint plethora poured;
In gallery men's pure mystique displayed.
No need to socialise, nor small talk utter.
Such flotsam in that ambience was nought,
Inane the banter, guarded truths men mutter;
I dreamed amongst belief in aspect caught,
Where the convoluted, nightmare whims escaped,
Quite beautiful despite the wounds that bled,
More clear perhaps than mountain paths landscaped,
Or still life with pear nudging loaf of bread
Purple play was not exclusively a storm,
Nor carmine cap the sun's own slumber crown,
I saw strident gold and black in tragic form,
Beheld a painter's pain in pigment drown
And I intimated, sotto voce 'I learn
To probe within the outward camouflage,
With art's ambiguous signals to discern;
One solo slant on life and no mirage.'
Flowed a finitude amok in artist's veins,
Sudden cynosure with light befriending
And a pioneering paint broke free from chains,
Brave palette petty thought transcending.

Ruth Daviat

NATURAL ART

Nature is an art unto itself
structure, colour, texture
such a lovely mixture.
Take the bark of a tree
to the smooth green leaves
or the red hot sun
with a cool gentle breeze.
The pampas grass
standing oh so bold
the small rose bush
as its petals unfold.
So if you look closely
'cause nature is smart
you'll see for yourself
it really is art.

Dorothy Johnstone

IMPRESSIONS OF THE IMPRESSIONISTS

Pierre-Auguste Renoir immediately comes to mind
'Bal du Moulin de la Galette'
And 'Luncheon of the Boating Party'
'Dancing in the Country' and 'Dancing in the Town'
'Young Girls at the Piano' then on to a sombre note
'The Umbrellas' each opal face with eyes that speak.

His friend Claude-Oscar Monet's 'Impression: Sunrise'
'Wild Poppies' and 'La Grenouillère' by the Seine,
'Regatta at Argenteuil', mystical scenes of London
And countless paintings of his garden at Giverny.
His caring friend Frederic Bazille's
'Monet after his accident at the Inn at Chailly'.

Another friend Edouard Manet's 'Luncheon on the Grass'
'Portrait of Emile Zola', 'Olympia'
And 'Bar at the Folies-Bergère'
His sister-in-law Berthe Morisot's 'The Cot' -
A mother ponders with wonderment,
And her charming scene 'Looking for Butterflies'.

A friend to them all - Henri Fantin-Latour's
'Portrait d'Edouard Manet' and
'A Studio in the Batignolles' -
A meaningful masterpiece
Of friends all together
A concentration of genius on one canvas!

Barbara Fosh

THE DANCING YEARS

I wonder how many really consider the enjoyment they get from dance,
And, having thought about it, realise that they achieve it not just by chance.
The steps they learn are taught by someone who has dedication and respect,
For they realise that although some are naturals there are the two
  left feet you would expect.
And then there are the ones who aspire to greatness, they have a talent
  to succeed.
Who if they can remain unaffected give the encouragement beginners need.
For when we begin to learn we feel we'll never get it right,
When we see the expert who never puts a foot wrong, we tend to
  get uptight.
If you're lucky enough to belong to a club that appreciates how we feel,
And has the patience to show that success can be very real.
The success is important, but if the club regards the social aspect
  it's a bonus.
For when people meet in a social way, it helps, and that applies to us.
We get the benefit of those who have given their whole life to
  teach.
There are festivals, etc, we can enjoy in the unique ballroom
  within our reach.
And so the whole becomes part of a lifestyle that's good for
  all of us.
We can dance, and pass the time with everyone with very little fuss.
An ambition is to carry on indefinitely and keep those feet tripping
  round the floor.
But when we have to give up there'll be happy memories with
  us for evermore.

Reg Morris

COOL THINKING

In Italy, most people sleep the sullen mid-day heat away,
but, here in England, many people say,
'How the Italians waste their lovely days.'

These people take their shorts and barrier creams,
with scant regard for heat exhaustion, so it seems,
into the blazing rays.

I long for pauses in humidity
and take myself to cool refreshing showers and thence to bed,
to clear my head and rest my aching bones -
accompanied by moans from friends and family -
but, as the evening comes, and others yearn for rest,
my best thoughts come.
I happily keep going,
knowing that, with cool night, my tread will lighten,
hoping for inspiration,
and shooting stars of insight into man's condition,
awaiting the chance to write.

Thus, thankfully, I bid the world, 'Sleep well . . . '
and then?
I keep the next appointment with my pen.

Viva siesta.

M C Wood

ONE OF THE ARTS

The 'Arts' consist, of many things,
  Such as drama, opera and dance,
But I like putting my thoughts in rhyme,
  Whenever, I have the chance.

'Cos I think, writing poetry, is relaxing,
  And is one of the fine arts,
With no need for rehearsals
  Before, you play the parts.

You just let, your memory wander,
  To the days, when you were young,
And it's surprising, how the words
  Start flowing, from your tongue.

I scribble poems, in my notebook,
  While I'm having a tea break,
And when my verses get published,
  It's the 'icing on the cake.'

Jean Hendrie

THE ONLOOKER'S DELIGHT

The white statue of the officer and horse
look cold as they stand very still.
Their attention is of course
to the palace and never will
be allowed to turn and fade.
The brushes used to make the colours
on the canvas are a pleasure
for the onlooker's delight,
and are done with time of day and moonlight,
making pictures of humans, buildings and river scenes.
The ballerina in her white satin and lace
with her steps on points
will make your heart race
as she makes a beautiful swan
on the silvery lake.
The stage is set for the pantomime.
The comics joke and the clown will fall.
We will applaud and have a good time
and shout encore! For another curtain call,
before travelling home again.
The writer tells a story in ink
of love, of life and work
the murder and mystery and the kitchen sink
the reader is so enthralled with the book
and reads it cover to cover before putting it down.
The poet writes a few lines
and hopes and prays
it comes out in rhymes.
He can say it will be alright
then wish you a really good day and happy goodnight.

R Medland

HARRIET

There is in art,
like a poet's words
a story meant to tell.

And this, this lady,
she aims to tell,
to write the words,
that soon will quell,
the words inside her,
and soon beside her,
you see her words so well

That she with her art, she does not part,
she works to make it pay,
that dark hair, and fine complexion,
and eyes that tell no lies,
she writes as her art does say.

But when for another, who wants to differ,
to her it is no bother,
she takes her brush, and with no rush,
she'll make the clothes that differ.

But she's prettier than the pictures,
she paints upon the clothes,
for the people proud, who stare aloud,
and look true upon the clothes,
and see but part, of that called art,
that's placed upon the clothes.

And who's this lady that should be met,
why, don't you know? It's Harriet!
It's her, and her alone,
who takes this art, and makes clothes apart,
the one from one another!

Osamah Gahin

HIDDEN DEPTHS

I believe that all people have a creative streak,
Often well hidden, until others get a peek.
Painting and poetry are usually solitary pastimes,
While drama and dance provide a social lifeline.
A few people have a natural talent,
Which cannot be acquired by others, or lent.
All forms of art provide a sort of escapism,
A move away from the present and realism.
Everywhere people look they're faced with modern creations,
Art provides an outlet for inner frustrations.
What people think and deeply feel they give out,
Various words and pictures loud messages shout.
Without numerous arts what would the world become,
An empty grey place, with people feeling glum.

Susan Mullinger

WORK OF ART

This is Jeannette Facchini
Artist extrordinaire,
One day in the art class,
Teacher said, 'There's talent there.
In that little corner,
Half an inch of fame,
I think it's quite remarkable,
The way you sign your name!'

J Facchini

POETIC ART

With words I create a picture,
No brush or paint for me;
But there is colour in how I write,
Such is the art of poetry.

Inspiration I will always find,
A combination of heart and mind,
When from my pen, such feelings flow,
That only a poet can ever show.

Eternally poets will strive to write,
Verses that bring such delight,
Those feelings from the very heart,
For poetry is a special art.

R Duck

TIME TO DREAM

Whilst staying with a friend of mine, a story I was told
Relating to her neighbour, a ballet star of old
We called around to see her, as my friend had got a key
To keep a constant vigil on the star that used to be

This once prima ballerina, of a now quite distant age
Was maybe dancing with the memories, of the time she graced the stage
She was very deep in slumber, with a smile upon her face
Her long since, not used, ballet shoes, proudly hung in pride of place

Was she dreaming of the bouquets of her nightly accolade
Or the gentlemen who once loved her, or of all the friends she made
Where are they now, I wondered as we left the fading star
Still dreaming of the days gone by . . . and her Swan Lake repertoire.

Bell Ferris

MIDDLE AGE

When work is thru' and chores are done
we should have time to make some fun
all duties cares and worries gone
relax, enjoy the time you've won.

Take up painting, sport or such
or flower arranging you love so much
perhaps you'd like to make a rug
or even a toy for a child to hug.

As long as you do have the time
fill your life even though in prime
the things you had to put aside
can now be done with joy and pride.

You have the time now the family's flown
whatever the choice, it's your very own
so ease up from that rocking chair
the snoozing and the devil may care.

Begin to live and enjoy your life,
the days are gone that were filled with strife
the time is now to begin again
enjoy the pleasure and forget the pain.

H Cullum

UNTITLED

A poet's art is quite a thing
choosing words to mingle in
painting pictures in pure thought
plucking emotional strings so taut

So why does he then waste his time
choosing all these words so fine
if only for his own amuse
or does he leave you with a ruse

There's poets and 'poets' of this I'm sure
what is it you're looking for
a romantic quip to lull the heart
or work that knows the meaning o' Art

Art is not for art's own sake
artists have a purpose to make
to transmit to the future land
pearls of wisdom held in hand.

Shaun Hopkins

THE ARTIST'S TALE

I was marching with the crowd
When a great voice cried aloud
'Come away, come away' and I obeyed.
'You were out of step and had you stayed
Among the throng you would have tumbled
And no-one, not one, would have humbled
Himself to raise you to your feet.
They cannot stop but must complete
Their journey. Each follows the man
In front, allowing others to plan
The route. They have no leader, yet
They cannot stray; their path is set.
But theirs is a way of no creation,
No vital spark of imagination.
The milling crowd is deaf and blind;
To join them you must stop your ears and bind
Your eyes. You must laugh when they laugh,
Cry when they cry; there can be no half-
Measures. If you choose their way you will be sure
Of acceptance. But your soul will not endure.
So, my friend, decide your fate,
Before you find it's much too late!'

Rose Worms

BALLET SHOES

Soft pink, as petal hyacinth
woven from hues
of simple delight.
To my feet
dancing shoes
carry me into dreams,
distant beauty,
snow-capped mountains
fade into mist.
Sea music in my ears
as waves beat on a shore,
dancing feet succumb
intermingled with pink hyacinth
petal dew, fairy light,
to my feet dancing shoes
each step an imprint
on my heart.

Joan Hands

APPRECIATE

Are you young
Are you old
Take a look and let the Arts unfold,
Say what you feel
Don't shy away
Open your eyes and heart today.

Are you rich
Are you poor
Who are the Arts really for,
Does it matter
Do we care
So long as we appreciate what's there.

T Read

ARTISTIC TRIALS

Writing, painting, drawing, acting
All demanding, all exacting
Artistry has a special chemistry
Lower depths and higher ecstasy.

Footsore, aching limbs of dancers
No room here for part-time chancers.
Failing light to hinder brushstrokes
Thought blockage for the writing folks.

The depths of despair
With absent flair
The peaks when all goes right
The deepest dark, the brightest light.

The time, a hard taskmaster
Setback makes it travel faster
Then the waiting, hoping, wondering
Success? Or would it be a floundering.

Yet with all its ups and downs
With all its causing furrowed frowns
An artist cannot forsake his sector
It's a compelling, driving, thriving nectar.

Danny Pyle

BON GIORNO - MADAM BUTTERFLY

In boyhood, when I sung in school, my *choirmaster* was most impressed
And told my parents - that with my *voice* - I could go far,
Later in wartime, in *Naples*, visiting *Italian officers*, heard me sing
And remarked - 'In *opera*, - this *British* soldier could become a star.

After *demob* - back to school in *London*, for *operatic training*,
To learn *deportment*, and *acting* - *on the* stage,
Then, at last - I knew that I was ready
To turn over - to the next page.

First - came an opening, for a temporary spot in *Swansea*
Their regular *tenor*, had been taken ill,
But, when I confessed - that I was not experienced
They said *Sorry* - I wouldn't fit the bill.

Suddenly from *Leeds*, for a role in *'La Boheme;*
Came a very welcome invitation,
I went - I sung - I was a success
With a full minute's standing ovation.

Then it all happened - in *Manchester*, I was in *'Manon'*
In *Glasgow* - I sung in the *'Pearl Fishers'*
It was wonderful - I had tasted success
And the taste - was really *delicious*.

At last - came a call from *Covent Garden*
They needed a *tenor* for the *'Italian Girl in Algiers'*
I sung there - as I've never sung before
To a tumult of *Applause* - *Bravo* - and *Cheers*.

So listen - *Senor Pavarotti* - *Domingo* - and *Carreras*
If you need a *holiday* - or decide to have the *'flu'*
Just remember - although you all have my *best wishes*
I am always ready, to step in - as your *No 2*.

Paul Gold

A STUDY ON PROSE

They'll call me uneducated I suppose
When ambling on about wandering prose,
But I don't think anybody really knows
Where it comes from or where it goes.

Kevin J Foulger

ART IS FOR ME

I missed out on hobbies
When I was a mum
But bringing up children
Was a whole lot of fun
I missed my vocation
For art was for me
I could draw on a whim
Trees or boats on the sea
Perhaps if I went to evening class
Brush up so to speak
On my favourite art
I love the country the green
And the trees
Or the seaside I'd paint
The sands and blue sea
Subjects and objects of every size
I could paint where I liked
Even stars in the night
Yes I'm convinced that
Painting's for me
In a few years from now
Who knows where I'll be
I could be famous
Sell paintings galore
At a gallery where people
Would queue at the door.

Jeanette Gaffney

A BUNDLE OF JOY

I see a bay encircling
Calm briny waters of aquamarine
tide-turned to kiss the hem of a clear sky blue kirtle
Mother Nature's fond greeting within the sound of the sea.
Marram grasses are defending white-faced sea campion
underfoot a carpet of yellow brassicas sunnily blooms
while boats in the bay are undoubtedly anchorin' -
a view from the stony cliff path that side-steps the dunes.

We chance to meet here the freshness of childhood
peachy of cheek with lips of cheeky red hues
she stands entranced high above the seashore
head bowed but shaded by a poke bonnet of soft blues.
A wave of fair hair drifts onto her forehead
plays soft at her neck concealing young shell-like ears
innocent eyes lowered in wonderment
her whole being absorbed in a scene that endears

Sweet girl of ten summers clad in black leggings
shod in black serviceable boots - sturdy the toe
sturdy the wearer - conversant with stony walkings
but a touch of dainty blue frilly is peeping below
homespun frocking - weathered like a dusty beachcomber
over which is worn a white shift of pinafore from an age long ago
the focus of her attention are in the folds of her pinny there
for she cradles two tabby kittens - 'A bundle of joy'.

Did she find them in the creel behind her basketed with straw
What is their story? Tabbycat knows - she offers a paw.
Abandoned or ship-wrecked the litter look in fine fettle
maybe they strayed inadvertently from the cot overlooking the bay
I expect they'll soon kiss the hem of a dear homely kirtle
returning Mother's fond greeting within the sound of the sea.

Lucy Green

POET

If I could be another me,
Then a poet I would love to be.
For they have a way with words,
They tell of trees, and flowers, and birds.
They tell of happiness and joy,
Of love between a girl and boy.
They speak of things you've never had,
And sometimes make you feel so sad.
Some poems are short,
And some are long,
Some for the old
And some the young.
But a poet I will never be,
I'll have to stay as just plain me.

J Stephens

ARTISTIC ENDEAVOUR

Is there more to life
than the pub and the bookies?
Eh, basket weaving and cookies.
Is there more to life
than football and beer?
Eh, Tiffany stained-glass and Edward Lear.

Aye, pub culture is hard to beat,
And it keeps a boy off the street.
  As for the arts and crafts;
Show me a tapestry of George Best
scoring a winning goal for Ireland!
Let me see your stained-glass depiction
of the Grand National!
Paint a water-colour of my arse!

So, you won't come along to the pottery class then?

Kenneth McPhee

DANCE

The shyness of a small child,
Can suddenly disappear,
As her feet take on a magic,
That wipes away the fear.

She steps out in rhythm,
As she takes centre stage,
And the theatre grows silent,
At this child's tender age.

She smiles in the spotlight,
She's as free as a bird,
And the melody inside her,
Can truly now be heard.

For a few lonely minutes,
She feels she's on air,
And her heart beats in time,
As her feet dance away.

She taps her routine,
To the audience's delight,
On this special occasion,
The show's opening night.

M Cook

WAITING...

I keep hoping that the postman
Will pop a letter through my door
To say my work's successful
The publisher wants more.

While I go on waiting
New ideas are in my head
Should I put them down on paper?
No! I think I'll wait instead

Now at last, here comes the postman
He's heading down this way
But wait! He's gone right past me
Oh well, another day

I have got to keep on writing
Till people read my verse
They may like, or even loathe it
Laugh and sometimes curse

But for now I am just waiting
Is it talent (or just luck)
To see the words you have written
Published in a book...

Gig

THE RIVER DANCE

The River Dance is superb
So slick, smart and reserved
Its clickety click
was ever so quick
So rhythmic
so terrific!

Michael Flatley so high battery
so precise and so graceful
so united in rhythm
with Jean Butler a fixed prism!

So rat-a-tat-tat
just like a fast bat!

Marie Barker

CLOISTER CONSPIRACY

Distinguished setting, parochial place,
Four sinister figures, hooded, no face,
Black robes swirling, sweeping the ground,
Two hands clasped, knuckles, tight-bound.

Brothers Angelo, Michael, da Silva and Pierre
Consider their ploy, their conspiracy share,
So many years since that dreadful day.
They plotted and killed kind Father O'Shay.

Michael reluctant, as was his wont.
Three steps behind expressing doubt,
Pierre at the end, guilty head bent,
Shutting off voices, his argument spent.

Such in the daytime, do they appear,
But shadows lengthening far more to fear,
The little group together as one,
Continue chicanery so long begun.

The deed so cruel was never forgiven.
Condemned wander, by remorse sorely driven.
When daylight dawns, they're back in position
To think they've moved - just supposition.

But ladies and gentlemen, students too,
Will you stay behind, when the organ's through
Or will you like me proper time depart,
Having experienced magnificent incredible
          wonder of art.

Grace Wade

BIO-POEM

A poet is like a good shepherd,
Steering wayward words along a path,
To tell how he or she lived and cared,
Or to amuse with something wild or daft.

And like that tender of beasts ovine,
Should some cherished one go missing,
He'll leave the rest, search for spoor or sign
Of that truant, to return 'neath his 'wing'.

A good poem is quality wine,
Able to roll about the tongue,
Permit reader to verbally dine,
And later, 'mongst friends, its praises are sung.

Perry McDaid

I GO TO THEM TO FIND THEIR SOULS

Your way of crushing the Arts
Is subtle. You strongly declare -
Whilst we are both listening to a particular programme;
Programme that interests me,
And you not fully;
Programme about . . . an atheist scientist maybe,
Who talks about . . . science naturally,
But says also that he likes Hume,
And that he listens to Mozart,
And Wagner -
You strongly declare
That science is all. Science
Is all. You and I don't always see eye to eye.
I say, coming from the amoeba I may be . . .
Coming from the amoeba . . .
But now, I'm here, living on Earth;
And I have to make sense of this fact;
Try to understand;
Create a life that I can cope with.
I say, I need
To listen to writers,
In total freedom.
I need to view paintings;
I need to let my heart feel; I change
Through the Arts -
I grow.
Artists speak to whatever it is in me, that . . .

They have a way of looking at things.
They make me see; they make much apparent.
I see how it could be.

Claire-Lyse Sylvester

ART'S MOST PRINCELY SHRINE

Art has her shrine in several things,
Poetry, music, sculpture, art,
She lives in drama too
Entertaining crowds with no to do.
She lives in every human sphere
Both up and down and east and west
And fits so snug in every clime.
The oriental temple fair
The great skyscrapers in New York
And roads entangled in LA.
The painting hanging on the wall
The piano sitting in the lounge
The bust upon the handsome plinth
The drama acted out by kids
Are all a part of her great lore.
But ah! The wealth of sheer delight
As love and I romp through each page
And play each mellow haunting tune
And stand serene in fond embrace
Or re-enact our favourite play.
But what surpasses nature's thrills
As we each murmur fonder verse
And play on our hearts' strings a tune
Or else replay our favourite pose
Or act life's dream upon life's stage.

Thomas W Splitt

STRATEGY

As I go on to the ice with my skates
I see the young falling and many
mistakes, strategy is what they need
as the adults look at their feet.
Listen everyone why are you hanging
on to the post? I'm scared! A child
voices out!
I will show you where you and many
others are going wrong!

What's your name? Juile! I'm Clair,
now watch the boy with his blue jersey
do you like the music? Yes! That's
why I come, motion is what you
need! Keep looking ahead. Do you,
notice something? No! But I'm skating
exactly. You're across the other side,
and they're still hanging on, as we
laughed.

Look! There's my older brother he's
skating with many others, oh!
as a boy falls, you see Juile!
The secret of skating is talking
to others and please do not
stop! Draw in, at the side if you
feel threatened, by the ones that
go over the top.

Monica R Rehill

MY DYING SWAN

Hush the crowd, a lifting cloud,
In shifting flight a veil flows white,
A fragile tremor draws the light,
Unmasks a slender glass pointe pose.

A wild impassioned elegance,
Becalmed beneath life's spell,
Beauty pains the heart that knows,
A flame remembered well.

Enchanted lightness charms the stage,
Weave the dreams and fairy tales.
Escape the fear; life's embers fade,
My shining Catherine wheel.

Already beauty's felt not seen,
Perfection drawn from instinct. Harmony,
And sheer strength of passion light her boundaries,
Fleetingly.

Music colours her dark world,
Draws life through her veins.
The swan distant, delicate, dying,
Blinds you to her pains.

What gently fades will weaken, crumble,
Slip away young heart so pained,
Dazzling brightness dimmed by fate,
Fluid beauty drained.

Forever in my aching heart,
I'll clasp your timeless image,
I watch through frosted light, held breath,
A silken magic sway, and once again,
You dance so beautifully into death.

Felicity Webster

CAKE CAPERS

Into the kitchen,
Find a pretty pan.
Mother has her apron on,
To cook with her you can.

Spread your little finger
On the dough to make a shape,
There's several sweety spices
You can sprinkle in your cake.

Reach up for the raisins,
The jar upon the shelf.
Throw a cluster in the mix
Then eat a few yourself.

Stir around the sugar,
Beat the eggs and cream.
Whip a frothy mixture,
It will fluff up like a dream.

While the oven's heating
Grease the pan around,
Swirling treacle, chocolate drops,
Whatever nice is found

In your little cupboard,
To make your cake a treat,
And when it's baked all soft and warm
Then call your friends to eat.

Marion Elizabeth Sherwood

THE MASTERS

Art will be with us for all time,
We had Constable and Turner,
The masterpieces of those artists,
Will inspire many a learner.

They did paint and capture the beauty,
Of surrounding countryside and trees,
Farmyards and animals brought to life,
With their brushes and paints, such expertise.

Each little blade of grass so perfect,
You can hear the trickle of the stream,
The strain of the cart horse dreying her load,
Such tranquillity shown in every scene.

Their paintings, so real, so alive,
Love of their work put into each brush stroke,
Trees swaying gently, in the summer breeze,
The thatched cottage chimney, billowing smoke.

There might be future greats at art school,
Striving for detail and perfection,
If they study and learn from the masters,
They will be headed in the right direction.

I don't mean they should copy, just feel,
Feel the love from their canvasses emanating,
Feel the emotions they put into their work,
See the pleasure they felt in their creating.

Many other great artists are immortalised,
Their legacies to us will always live on,
Capture the beauty of life in your work,
As sadly, the scenes of the masters are now gone.

Glennis Horne

THE ARTS IN NATURE

Nature has its own canvas
on which a picture to make
She gloriously shows her colours
reflecting the sky on a lake

The trees in autumn are dressed in red,
in yellow and deepest gold
and snow, lying peaceful and pristine white
is a beauty to behold

Nature does not need an orchestra
just listen to the birds as they sing
The blackbird, the robin, the nightingale
or wild geese as they call, on the wing

Nature does not need a ballet
a fox-trot or waltz
watch the corn dance watch the grass sway
as the wind just takes its course

Life is but a stage, it's said
and this is very true
for there is such beauty all around
a theatre for me and you

Jenny Brownjohn

THE FORGOTTEN MANUSCRIPT

The manuscript lies unopened
Hiding the notes that are written within.
Dusty, neglected brown with age
The composer's name just visible upon the front.
Too late for him to realise his fortune or his fame.
The piano lid is shut, protecting the ivory keys
Faded, unpolished, forgotten,
The tapestry stool sadly threadbare
A lone music stand cast upon the floor
As if in a time capsule waiting to evolve.
A shaft of sunlight pours across the darkened room
A bidding to awaken the musician's skill
Music of a distant age.
Counterpoint - intermingled sounds
Years of lonely dedication waiting to unfold.

Anne Christabel Davey-Young

CARDIACS BEST BAND IN THE WORLD

I was bored with
Normal music
And jungle and Techno
Made me feel sick
I went to a gig
The Cardiacs were there
I heard a tune
This is it I thought yeah!
I went to the shops
And found their albums
I let people hear the songs
Cardiacs' music
Astounds them
So thanks Tim, Jim, Jon
And Bob
From a fan just saying
Keep up a good job

Stephen Adams

DEDICATION OF A BALLERINA

When she was just three,
a ballerina she wanted to be.
To dance like a fairy was her desire,
and her ambition grew like a fire.

Ballerina sways like a tree,
Ballerina glides so gracefully.
She dances on pointed toes across the floor,
the audience calls out encore, encore.

Agile leaping like a gazelle,
dainty like a butterfly.
Every muscle, taut in flight,
Ballerina, this is your night.

You've waited many years for this moment,
to dance a leading role,
and now you have succeeded.
Ballerina you have reached your goal.

At the top of your profession,
you take the centre stage.
Flowers in arms, tears fall,
your name now famous in the hall.

Kathrine Summers

SWAN LAKE

The house lights dim, the curtains rise,
The dancer bathed in light,
In sparkling, pure white tutu,
She is Odette tonight.

As graceful as the swan that she
Portrays in this sad story,
She pirouettes on fairy feet
To dance her way to glory.

Swan maidens gather round her
To offer their protection,
The magic scene upon the stage
Is one of sheer perfection.

Her handsome prince now enters, they
Perform their pas-de-deux,
He lifts her, holds her, all can see
That he's in love with her.

The tale unfolds, but can his love
Release his Swan Princess?
To take her as his blushing bride
His life alone, to bless.

Alas, for him, 'twas not to be,
The audience knows that's true,
They just enjoy the dancing,
As ballet lovers do.

The show is over, and Odette
Accepts the adulation
Of people rising to their feet,
A well-deserved ovation.

Margaret Curzon-Howe

HASLAND THEATRE COMPANY'S
50TH ANNIVERSARY: 1946 - 1996

It's fifty years and many shows -
Since first enthusiasts brought a glow,
To ardent playgoers living near -
With five productions staged each year!

From small beginnings we are proud
Of early efforts - and are loud
In our praise of all their work -
That results in such a perk!

Yet times have changed - and now we own -
Our Local Theatre - that has grown,
With care and loving efforts made -
So many talents on parade!

Drama, farce and panto too -
Compete for favour - as they do!
Growing stronger with each day -
Entertaining, seasonal play!

For in this Anniversary Year -
As Mayoral guests enjoy good cheer!
We thank supporters - old and new -
And hope our future's sound and true!

For living theatre does uplift,
All our lives - and is a gift -
To spread abroad the joy we feel,
At Hasland Theatre Company zeal!

Doreen Wheeldon

CREATIVE ART

If all new-born were artists
they'd watch wavelets draw pictures in sand
and butterflies flying in woodland
defining space through indigenous trees
they'd hear bees tell what business really is
grasshoppers tuning their music to the gentle breeze

If all new-born were artists
painters poets sculptors and musicians
would be superfluous
for art in all its green and glorious creation
would be seen and heard just everywhere.

Pat Mear

ART

Oh God gave man the gift to plan
Ambition, life and learning;
And various arts play differing parts
To help him strive to bring alive
The substance of his yearning.

The devil shifts to use God's gifts
If man will play his part.
In godless states, where he dictates,
Distortions and indiscipline,
Pornography and blasphemy
Are still considered art.

When man's inclined to speak his mind,
His inner self confessing.
We question whether it's altogether
Our part to sniff or praise; or if
His ego's worth expressing.

Technique is yet remaining, and a man must do his training
Before he acts, composes, paints or writes;
But the soul of every art lies within the human heart . . .
The battleground where saint with devil fights.
In a world that's come unstuck must we wallow in the muck?
Or inspire mankind with more salubrious flights?

Simon Peterson

ARTS AND CRAFTS

I wish I knew the reason why
My crafty efforts go awry.
Misshapen pots adorn my ledges
While wobbly tables rest on wedges,
And trailing plants hang in profusion
To hide macramé in confusion.

I donned my wellies and my mac
And ventured forth with haversack
To gather ferns and woodland sprays
To cheer my home through wintry days;
But alas, my autumnal art
Withered and drooped and fell apart.

There's canework soaking in my sink
But the intended lampshade will I think
Serve to keep waste paper in,
(If I can fit it with a bin).
I've tried my hand at making lace,
Resulting tangle's a disgrace!

There must be something I can do,
Something relaxing, something new!
The time has come for a fresh start,
I'll take up classes in real art,
Maybe I have the artistic touch
And paint and brushes won't cost much.

Jean M White

LINK

Putting pen to paper,
Using words to express,
Whether rhyming or not,
Feelings, moods and situations,
Places and faces,
Giving inner satisfaction,
Seeing it all in print,
Putting brush to canvas,
Colourful pictures from the mind's eye,
Scenes that in mere words can't be told,
Lines that stand out so bold,
Putting the two together a powerful drama for the stage,
An appreciative audience,
Acting our words and pictures,
A combination of characters and scenery,
For all to enjoy,
Portraying comedy and tragedy,
The ultimate coming together,
A spellbound audience,
A play on stage,
That could become all the rage,
Just reward for hours a graft crafting the pieces to become one.

D L Redman

MAYBE ONE DAY ...

The very first time that I entered a rhyme
In a locally run competition,
My efforts were spurned and my work was returned
And it dented my writing ambition.

But 'try, try again' is the age old refrain;
I decided to give it a go.
So I sent in some more but, just as before,
They dealt me another cruel blow.

I spend all my time chasing rhythm and rhyme
But somehow they seem so elusive.
It's not good enough churning out this old stuff,
I need something really exclusive.

Original themes are my hopes and my dreams,
But how do I find inspiration?
I've searched round my brain and I've searched it again
But I think that it's in hibernation.

My brain is decaying. I need a good saying
To help me accept it with grace.
So what I propose is that 'As one door closes
Another one slams in my face!'

The poem I write seems alright on the night
That I write it. There's lots of 'me' in it.
I send it away but the very next day
Some young upstart's decided to bin it!

I've tried and I've tried, been so sad that I've cried.
Dogged by ill fortune for years.
I try to write verse but my efforts get worse
And everything's ended in tears.

I'll try just once more to be published before
I'm too feeble to pick up a pen.
As posthumous fame may establish my name,
But I'll be past caring by then!

Dennis Turner

DAY DREAMER

Your eyes are closed yet you can see
There are pictures in your head
Visions of things that you could be
Hearing things that would be said

No obstacles to mar your way
Your destiny looked so clear
Believing everything you say
In your mind you have no fear

The play is yours to command
A hero if you choose to be
Things just fall to hand
In visions only you can see

So vivid it all looks real
You only have to touch
It's as though you can feel
Freeze frame if it gets too much

To look back you just rewind
It's like pictures in a book
A film set in your mind
Where only you can look

In a theatre that is your own
You can be a hero or a schemer
Take trips into the great unknown
For you are an old day dreamer

Roy Hunter

TAP DANCING

Have you ever experienced real tap dancing?
It's an experience to remember, it's better than anything.
I can remember when I had my very first tap class,
I was three years old and I thought I was the best.
A pair of tap shoes was given to me,
the sound of tappers tapping was just so heavenly.
I also remember my first tap step I really was so proud,
I took my very first exam and passed without a doubt.
Exam after exam I passed all the time,
I rarely get the chance but when I do it is so fine.
The examiner comes in, my nerves start to go,
I think about the certificates but I don't let it show.
Now I'm fifteen and I have moved on,
I've gone to a new school now that is number one.
I've also taken up a new style of dancing,
but every-one knows tap is really the best thing.

Kerry Louise Hayley (15)

COULD IT BE..?

Could it be
That I'm the only one
To see that tree?

Do I alone
Hear its leaves rustle
And its branches moan?

Can it be
That its scent falls
Not on you but me?

Do only I
Caress its soft bark
With a gentle sigh?

Is it only me
Who tastes the fruit
That feeds the bee?

Can you see
That what I feel
Belongs to me?

Yet, it is true
That the song I sing
Is meant for you.

Stan Morton

ART OR COMMERCE

I would have loved to write,
but finances were tight;
I had to concentrate on my career.
I should have learned to dance,
but did not take the chance
of letting such distractions interfere.
I had a mind to act,
but fear of being sacked
meant working every hour of my leisure.
I could have trained my voice,
but had to make a choice
twixt business and pursuit of any pleasure.
It plainly can be seen
the success that I have been,
slaving in my office every night.
But now in my old age
it's very hard to gauge
quite whether my priorities were right.

Malcolm Brown

WORK OF ART

Many years ago the world
of arts began,
Great writers knew what
to do,
they must have thought these
things through.

Shakespeare he wrote some good
plays,
A scholar who did his
best in those days.

Now he is remembered throughout
the land
People of today think his work
is grand.

Nicola Regan

ART V SCIENCE

Science has boundaries, limitations of physical laws,
discovered or yet to be found.
Even the Creator had to bend before such rules
in order to encompass and contain
the products of that Creation.
But Art has no such restrictions or laws;
only the walls of the imagination can hold Art back,
and confine it. For Art is a re-creation
from the bottomless depths of the mind -
a reflection, perhaps, of the aspirations -
freed from the gravitational pull of necessary Science -
of the Creator.
We have within ourselves the ability to create -
through dance, through drama, through paper, pencil, paint,
metal, clay and words, through notes of music,
echoes, maybe, of an unreasoning, unearthly heaven or hell . . .
Through all these things we can find the means to express
the individual or joint beliefs, truths, knowledge, wisdom, beauty,
or their opposites -
unbound by reason or physical laws.
Through all these things we may find and bring to the surface
the unplumbable depths and irrepressible expression
of human imagination;
the great and glorious freedom -
and vagaries and variances -
unrestrained by rules and regulations -
within a single human mind.

J Margaret Service

MASTER CLASS

With steady steps though,
No longer in the prime of life,
This veteran of poetic grace,
Whose skill and expertise,
Now passed on to youth,

Where once the body free,
In self expression of this art
As feather light with grace,
Each pirouette, a spiral of delight,
And arabesque of symmetrical beauty,

A crescendo reached deafening applause,
With standing ovation,
Roses scattered across the stage,
From enthusiastic admirers,
Of the dedication a prima alone holds,

Bouquet against skirt of frothy tulle,
Satin bodice wet with sweat,
The stick raps the floor,
To an assembled class of hopefuls,
Clad in uniformity,

Pink satin upon the feet,
Arching in releve',
All in perfect synchronous harmony,
Bodies leap through the air,
In jete' of tremendous height,

This master who demands perfection,
Who accepts not less,
Will once more a prima mould,
Until life's final curtain calls,
Her take a bow.

Ann G Wallace

THOUGHTS

For those we've loved,
The sentiment,
For those we love,
The giving,
For those who've gone,
The memory,
For those we've left,
The living.

Brian George Wellsbury

THE MODERN ANTHOLOGY

When I read another anthology
I feel pleasure, then despair,
For I'm certainly no Shakespeare
And I'm not as funny as Lear.

These modern poets are clever,
A really knowledgeable lot,
There's no limit to their prowess,
So what chance has this simple soul got

Of churning out some poetry
That has a touch of finesse,
Which will also tug at folks' heart-strings
And not end up in a mess?

I know they say all we poets are mad
Still my words come from the heart,
I'll never be Christina Rossetti,
Or Byron, or Kipling or Smart,

But just another modern poet
Feeling her way in the dark,
(The daffodils have been written about
And, drat it, so has the lark!).

So, it's back to reading the anthology
That is full of culture, wit and despair,
Some gloriously entertaining reading
(And some that tears at the hair!)

Well, time now to put pen to paper
To let you know what *I* can do,
On second thoughts maybe it's better
To take myself off to the zoo . . .

Gwynn Watt

THE SCHOOL'S HOUSEHOLD MUSICIANS

From practice-room doorways wind melodic trills
Of notes when new pieces reach learning's last stages,
Not for other teachers or parents to hear, till
The whole concert programme engages.

These pupils use their talent without apology
For anybody; and troop home in early
Starlight from rehearsals, where pure mental energy
Creates tone-worlds bejewelled and pearly.

The same old assembly hall grand gives a note for
A madrigal; while sheet music, in sliding piles
Threatens to tumble. The music great men wrote
Comprise the most elegant styles.

Gillian Fisher

THE PICTURE

The painting doesn't look a bit like me
But she assures me it is - wish I could see
Through her blue eyes how I appear to her
'Cos to me, what I see, is only a blur!

'Look - there's your mouth and there's your eyes
This is your nose' - my, how she sighs.
Her brow is furrowed in deep concentration
The paint's applied with great deliberation.

A swirl of yellow represents my hair -
I'm a peculiar shape, but I don't care!
My shoes are a really lovely black blob -
She's doing such a wonderful job!

I ask 'What's that?' - 'It's your bag' she replies
As a stroke of red paint is swiftly applied.
She studies her picture - why can't I see
That it really does look a lot like me?

The paintbrush is held suspended in air
Should I interrupt her - should I dare?
Artists can be so temperamental -
Best leave her alone - best be gentle!

Now she's looking at me to ensure it's complete -
This is going to be a really 'great' treat!
The picture's now finished and is given to me
By my youngest daughter - she's only just three!

Mary Buckingham

CLASSIFIED

What does art mean in the first instance?
Between object and life
is there a difference?
The concept of art
by its nature
Indefinable;
Just this,
No rewards, its mere existence is desirable.

What does art do in the second instance?
Does it touch one's life
and make a difference?
Look at your home,
At your street,
At your country,
Show me an object that escaped creativity!

Who makes art in the third instance?
Is movement a dance,
Is speech a deliverance
of text,
Like an act on the stage of experience.

Art must be everything if it is to succeed,
What differs with each of us is the ability to read
The signs that are given to show us that
Hey!
Art is life at the end of the day.

Emma Grainger

PUB TALK
(The Sculptor and Scientist)

'That sounds great! - pause - So it was a drawing showing this idea?'

'No it was real! They were actually there.'

'Well you've got to ask what is art? Don't you. Where is the skill in that?'

'You thought it was a beautiful idea, so why can't you accept the actuality which allows a total phenomena. The physical experience of an idea.'
'I could do that!
Anyone could do that!
There's no skill in that!'

'Anyone wouldn't do it though would they?'

'It's not art!'

'But you said it was a beautiful idea. This allows for an actual emotional response to the real situation. Rather than it just remaining an unrealised concept.'

'Manipulating people's feelings and emotions is cruel. I don't think that controlling someone's senses in an environment can be considered art!'

This is the essence of all art forms; music and poetry cause emotional response. Music is probably the most powerful, it can move you to tears. It is very rare that visual art can be so powerful.'

'Yeah that is true.'

We leave the bar and head to a late night cafe.

'If notes as music and words as poetry are art and I agree they have ability to trigger your emotions perhaps what you describe can also be considered art.'
'It would be interesting if artists tried to use science in art.'

'They do, the piece we first discussed is a perfect example.'

Long exploratory discussion.

'Well science is an art.'

'And art is a science!'

Matthew Walmsley

MALL
(And Jude)

Hasn't the dream? Slipping from be flat to another solution,
Freed your twisted limb from the ice of hallucination.

A lilac frock curls in light relining a wide lycra swoop,
The solace in seeing a head-of-pearl on the ice below.

'. . . see if there's any milk for coffee you.'
(Later you'll find his cam'ed-up head on ice in the Zanussi.)

Even a nod somewhere flat is a demand for the clockwise.
All you need do is make lazy white patterns in the mall.

Kevin Henderson

ART AND GALLERIES

In the same way that the Sabbath was made for each man,
I believe Art and Galleries need to be replanned.
We shouldn't make art around the design of the galleries,
Just so our hard work can increase their salaries.
The galleries should be shaped around the Art that we make,
Then all shall be happy as the Art won't be fake.

William FitzHugh

METAMORPHOSIS!

Heated day, on the wane; cool evening, taking hold;
Bess, (my dog) and I, sat on the fen, in a peaceful fold!
Obscured setting sun, inflamed, the darkening sky;
Breezes blowing; warmth, still in, supply!
Daylight, giving way, for opposition; a full silver moon;
Meditation began dominance, as silence, befell natural room!
Scorched grasses, reflected light; bush, shrub and tree;
Formed many, imaginative shape, for eyes, to see!
Winged amphibian, performed, a final circular flight;
Before retirement, for the coming night!
Periphery street illumination, took starlight form;
To carry forward, 'til released, by dawn!
Natural stars, slowly, made their, presence known;
As night, constructed, its temporary home!
Petalled wildflower, show, like a bridal miss;
To be married, by a dewy, midnight kiss!
The sights, that I see and give pleasure, to me;
Donated by nature, perfectly free!

Robert Denham

WRITER'S URGE

I have found nothing more threatening
Than a blank page staring up into my soul.
Patiently waiting,
Yet instilling insistence in me.
I hasten to fill the void
Knowing that if it stared long enough
An uncomfortable silence
That must be filled.
Maybe among the many dribbles and doodles
A mastery emerges.
Like an unfinished collage of the mind.
There I lay bare between
Silken sheets waiting to be
Revealed
By roving, lover's fingers.
Leafing through my life.
The page is filled with crossed off lines
And poetry re-done.
Angry red marks where
Mind and hand refuse to agree
And allow imagination to reign free.
I punish myself, I push myself
To fill in one more line.
There! This page is full to my content.
The next day, next page.
To be done.

Mariella Cassar

CUP OF TEA

Artists are just ordinary people.
Like anyone else,
They have to put,
Notes out to the milkman,
Scratch their private-parts,
Go to the Cashpoint,
Get more notes,
(But not for the milkman).

Painters like covering,
Blank surfaces with marks.
So, a note to the milkman,
Is a Big Event.

Maybe, that's the difference.

Barbara Hepworth couldn't get through the day,
Without a cup of tea.
Elgar wouldn't have produced,
His *Cello Concerto (adagio moderato)*,
If it wasn't for,
The milkman.

Steve Taylor

THE ARTS

The black arts
The artist who uses black ink
Who slashes with his pen
The writer who understood
The American crisis of identity
Which is as true for Bill Clinton
Seventy years later
One has to be very strange
To be an artist
An artist reaches out
To touch a spot
Unidentifiable to other people
When he points it out
They can't bear to acknowledge
What they see
Turn on the artist
Vilify him
So the artist draws a line
If he's any good
Few will understand
His achievement
Rather it is like
A slow lancing wound
That others carry in them
Fixed on paper or canvas
Everything stops there
He has made his point
The editor says
I'm not including him
As he's . . .

Natasha Ward

VISUAL ARTS

The arts, as a subject's quite immense;
Drama, music, literature have a voice,
Also the visual arts in abstract sense
And these I comment on by choice,
As words and sounds are rare in these.
Since modern works diversified
The esoteric few to please,
Dadaists, Fauves and Cubists vied
With surrealism and arts minimal,
But folk prefer familiar things,
Pictures of castles, landscapes, animal,
Portraits of history, queens and kings.
Granted its fun to mess and spoof,
Paint eyeballs on a nether end
Or put a whale upon a roof,
Art fights to satisfy the trend,
Above all else creative be,
Obscure, controversial and oblique,
Don't make a tree look like a tree,
But paint it like some nature's freak
To make a conversation piece,
And entertain the critics too
Whose intellect must never cease
To damn the old and praise the new.
We ponder form and things organic,
Or sculpture in its weirder guises
And wonder with a kind of panic
Why bricks and half a calf win prizes?

Donald Burt

DEAR POET LAUREATE

Dear Poet Laureate,

Please be careful what you say
If you criticise my work you'll spoil my bloody day,
I know you are at the pinnacle of your art
Please, go on, give my day a bloody good start.
We're not all as good as you are
And if you carry on - I won't get very far,
Dear Poet Laureate please be nice today
And put some helpful hints my way,
And don't criticise the way you've done of late,
Stop gobbing off and getting quite irate,
Stop and think sir, just for a little while,
We're both entitled to our own - style!
Dear Poet Laureate I'm sorry if I offend
I've also got my own style, I'll get there in the end.
And now I've got this poetic matter off my chest
I'll say farewell sir, and wish you all the best.

Afur Mo

LITTLE BALLERINA

My little girl
With hopes and dreams
And eyes so full of stars,
Life isn't always
As it seems
The road you tread is far.
The Ballet beckons,
Calls to you,
Your gift inborn, so pure,
Be careful child as off you dance
Towards the voice, be sure.
Be sure that it is all you want,
The path is hard and long,
With joy and tears along the way,
My graceful child, be strong.
Be strong and know that I am proud,
No matter how you do,
Your home is always waiting here
My arms outstretched to you.

Irene Carter

THE KISS
(Rodin)

Tenderness exudes
from pores of naked stone.
How natural they are together,
lovers bending to each other's bodies
and desires,
the gentle touch, the leaning curve
to completion.
Youthful figures
in a sharing of attraction,
timeless coupling.
They do not need to ask:
the kiss comes unbidden,
because it is so.

Marian Reid

AN ENGLISH ARTIST

In the Louvre there hangs a picture -
Look at the child with the cherries;
There is such beauty in her face
And what very tempting cherries,
Soft to touch, and red as berries,
They must have had delicious taste,
But for John Russell's clever brush,
She would be known to none of us.
Sweet little girl of long ago,
Your basket hold, your cherries show
Look at the child with the cherries.

G A Burgess

CREATIVE ART, I I LOVE YOU

I paint watercolours and draw
I send them to London galleries,
just imagine them hanging in
different houses, looked at by
people with blue eyes like sky,
green eyes like grass, brown
eyes like glass.

Kenneth Mood

ART GALLERY

Others have admired before you.
A minute's watchful pause is quite in order.
The frame should reassure you -
With confidence you may accord a second glance.

Slow down to circumambulate
That twisted figure.
If you appreciate its impact
We'll not snigger -
It has a label.

Let's leave the picture gallery behind us
And wander with no pedestals to guide.
The memory of those frames can still remind us
That beauty only bids us step aside
To find us.

Eleanor Nesbitt

WRITER

The writer can be a righter,
Please don't get it wrong,
Words make a idealistic fighter,
A weapon for the very strong.

To write, what is right,
Establishing every word,
With a warrior's might,
A battle cry seldom heard.

A pen mightier than the sword,
A knight with dictionary shield,
Marching across paper forward,
Into battle words don't yield.

Les Merton

SAWBRIDGEWORTH MUSICAL YOUTH THEATRE

Joining SMYT,
Was the best thing I've done in ages,
It gives me pleasure,
Every time I'm there,
Doing all the things I love,
Being with the people I like,

The happy times spent,
The fun and the laughs,
Friends I have made there,
Shows I have done,
People who've helped me,
The confidence I've gained,

Music and singing,
Fun and games,
Meeting new people,
Learning new things,
Chances of a lifetime,
And working with professionals,

The excitement you feel,
Each time the curtain rises,
The buzz you get when the audience clap,
Wearing silly costumes,
Thanking all the crew,
SMYT is the place to be.

Lynsey Bessent

SPICE OF LIFE

The world of the arts takes many talented people.
To get on the stage and reach their highest steeple.
A love of performing is what is required.
As actors are jolly and never seen tired.
Many great moments are shared from a play.
It's lovely to watch both night and by day.
A series on telly as in a soap.
Will always gain viewers, with plenty of hope.
Painters and models all love what they do.
For they know it gives pleasure for me and for you.
Then world of the arts is a fascinating thing
For there is always something that will give us a sting.
It's strange and it's wonderful both at the same time.
The wonder of the silence, when performing a mime.
It's here for eternity it's good and it's fun.
The many new avenues have yet not begun.

Trevor Barnes

DANCING

Dancing is a form of art
It brings a lot of pleasure
It's healthy exercise to take
When you have some leisure.

Many different styles of dance
Are there for you to choose
Be it ballroom, Irish, Scottish
Or line dancing to the blues

As you trip the light fantastic
Your spirits start to rise
Keep the rhythm going
Head up now, use your eyes

Then there's country dancing
Which goes back to days gone by
Make up sets of six or eight
You'll love it if you try.

You'll become enthusiastic
Will want to learn much more
The more you dance you'll happier be
Than you ever were before

Some come on, don't be bashful
I am sure you'll find it fun
Take a partner, have a go
The night is still yet young.

Verity Denton

NO OVERTURE

There is no overture to art, no time
Of introduction whilst the painting grows
To fullness and the viewer slowly knows -
As with the steps of melody or rhyme -
What fired the painter's brush. Sublime
On first encountering the eye, art flows
Directly past the questions thoughts impose
And nestles like an arrow in its prime
Recipient, the heart.
My words belong
To time and space and stumble through their praise,
Whilst even birds need sequence for their song;
But paintings come as lovers come, down ways
That know no future, right or wrong,
And give of their abundance as we gaze.

Mary Spain

AMBITION

If only I could play
The violin, viola
Or even the pianola,
To create a tune
Even try to croon.
I must do something in the arts,
Try for acting parts?
Attempt ballet
You know, Swan Lake,
A floral centre-piece
To make,
Or sculpt a figure fine,
Oh what dreams are mine,
An artist soon to be.
Move on please, Rodin,
To make way for little *me!*

Freda Tester-Ellis

THE DANCE FROM THE PAST

'To dance, I want to dance,' she said,
So they sent her away to learn.
They paid through the nose,
She stood on her toes
And did hip thrusts and posé turns.

She worked so hard; she made them proud,
She smiled and glittered and shone.
It was awful at home
But they took out a loan
And the dance, the dance went on.

And then a boy came sauntering by
And sadly turned her head.
Now she stood on *their* toes,
Still they paid through the nose,
But the dance, the dance was dead.

She went, just the same, to college each day
But the glitter and sparkle had gone.
It was 'Adam and Eve',
'I don't care if I leave!'
And the loan repayments went on.

They loved her and wanted her happy, so now
She dances a bit on the side.
But the 'thing' in her life
Is being a wife.
She is tied as all women are tied.

And still they love her and still they care
And they hope that she's happy at last.
But every day
What she threw away
Comes to haunt her - The Dance from the past.

Valerie Sutton

ACTORS

Actors,
Living out a part,
Up there,
Smiling on the stage,
Hiding broken hearts,
For a brief, short while, creating fantasy.

Brightening up, the public's life,
Living for applause.

They must keep on going, never, ever, pause.

Speaking words, of others, hiding all their fears,

Laughing, all the while,
Choking back their tears,

We applaud, and go into the night,

And never give a thought, to the pain,
Behind the stage spotlight.

Gladys Gayler

THE MASTER ARTIST

The finest artist you will ever meet, displays his work on every street,
In every field and in the meadow, upon the hills and in the hollow,
On mountains high sweeping down to the see,
The beauty of his work is for all to see,
Just look at the perfection of a rose,
Painted so perfect so that it glows,
Masses of colour, red, yellow and white,
Only a master can create this sight,
The hills and fields call colours of green,
Against purple mountains are a wonderful scene,
Every animal be it large or small
Birds and butterflies, little things that crawl,
Every shape and every size,
A kaleidoscope of colour, all with different eyes,
Who could have painted all this perfection,
A masterpiece in every direction,
This beauty for us, for ever will stay,
And the master artist is to whom we pray.

Michael Morris

OF LIFE AND ART

The velvet curtain opens wide at last,
The shadows dance and flicker on the screen,
Current events and things which are long past,
Ideals and images, produced and seen.

Seen as the play gives life to words and thought,
The spoken eloquence of verse and prose,
Ending with lessons learned and lessons taught,
Drama on ordinariness, its art bestows.

The paintings on the backdrop scenery,
Enchant the eye into a magic land,
Far from the strangle hold of grim reality,
Where dreams are possible and hopes are planned.

The words that dance and music bring to mind,
Emotions stirred by action or by song,
The comedy that may be cruel or kind,
Yet brings relief and helps the day along.

Yet do these arts all need appreciation,
Those who observe and so participate,
Giving the art 'street cred' and stimulation,
Listen with interest and sit and wait.

So is all art forever intertwined,
Bound by that need for creativity,
To share a thought inside another mind,
To be a part of all humanity.

Kathleen Scatchard

EMILY HATCH

I watched with pride my little girl
In her ballet dress
Step onto the platform
The judges to impress

With made-up face and hair in curls
And a sparkle in her eye
I could not believe how brave she was
She's usually very shy

I smiled at her, a watery smile
When she looked at me
Such a pretty little girl
My daughter Emily

Brenda Allen

WORDS

I switch off the light to the world outside,
Seeking out a place within.
Where memories are stirred, and words collide,
Sentence forming, I now begin.

To feel the words, hear the cry,
Thoughts to process, how and why?

This state of mind, I submerge into,
Words of old, ways of new.
Visualise with me, the words on the page,
Share in their laughter, love, dislike and rage!

Words are powerful,
The tools of my trade.
Relish their diversity,
For they're not easily made.

Tania Varndell

THE DANCER

Feel the rhythm feel the beat,
Hear the tapping of his feet,
He can shimmer he can shake,
Until he makes his body ache,
He can rock and he can roll,
He's got music in his soul.

Carolyn Finch

BALLET

A dance's spectral fable told
Set in Scotland's rural fold
Gave a sylph a dream remade
Led away was James' shade.

Unrequited love though kind
Was of sham's mere tainted side
So a dreamer saw an ilk
An ideal not harnessed silk.

Ae fond kiss was lastly seen
Under lights of bluey beams
Giving bias stunt and form
Not repeating Burns' forlorn.

David Bennett

MY PICTURE

I see the work of art in all the beauty
Of nature that is about - I see a tree that the
Artists dream to paint and place in a frame of gold -
And then more beauty to the painter's eyes - clouds
Forever moving in a sky of heavens blue - the
Painter sees it all - but only God can make it all
To appear before the eyes.

R P Scannell

THE SKATERS

How beautifully they glide across
the ice rink, as they dance,
The skaters, poised so gracefully,
in costumes their forms enhance.

They surely practise hours each day
perfection to achieve,
Such unison of movement
as complicated figures weave.

As swiftly o'er the ice they move
free skating with great skill,
Their footwork blending perfectly
to watch them is a thrill.

The music swells and echoes
there is magic in their blades,
As twisting, twirling, turning,
they always score high grades.

Attractive axles they perform
as round the rink they race,
Triple jumps and dizzy spins
executed so with grace.

Perfect artistry they share
for the world has seldom seen
Ice champions so talented
As Jayne Torvill and Christopher Dean.

Joan Heybourn

THE ART OF CREATING

We can all enjoy beautiful things
But creating is better still.
Just look at the rainbow up in the sky,
Your senses - it will fill.

We use the arts to express ourselves,
There's lots of different kinds.
For aesthetic value to touch the soul;
Let's open our hearts and minds.

A beautiful swan sculptured from ice,
Perhaps an arrangement of flowers.
A concerto composed to calm the nerves,
Or while away the hours.

You've something to say, you feel inspired,
The passion is a-burning.
You write a song to cheer folk up,
For the road that's twisting and turning.

Let's take a leaf from the Master's book,
And see what He has done.
And give some hope to a mixed-up world;
In beauty, we'll all be one.

Anne Black

ALL IN THE NAME OF ... ART!

My artistic ambitions took hold of me at a very early age.
Using dad's borrowed library books, I'd draw a masterpiece on each page!
By the age of ten I was *in* to fully unclothed nudes,
These varied not only in size and shape, but in myriads of vibrant colour!
Dad smiled at my attempts to shock saying, 'You'd best hide these from
                                                                    mother!'
Through teenage adolescence hormones going berserk, spotty, broody and
Artistically moody, temperamental, my painting was rather experimental!
Dad said, 'Draw a picture for me, a nice one, sort of sentimental.'
I went through Picasso's blue period, cubism, was saddened by his Guernica.
I wanted us all to move to Paris! Left bank of course, be famous, eureka!
Then I thought I mighty try sculpting, do a *Frink* horse, or a Henry Moore?
Mum said until my hormones settled down I'd never be too sure!
I fell madly in love at seventeen, gorgeous *Greg* from the *Tech,*
I told dad we were artists, kindred spirits, he said, 'Oh heck!'
Love faded fast when he left me for his *delicious* Dierdre Mintoff,
I threw myself into a frenzy of painting in anguish, sun flowers, just
Like poor old Van Gogh!
Dad said they hurt his eyes, 'And don't go cuttin' your ear off!'
He bought books on Monet, Gaugin, Renoir, and Toulouse Lautrec,
A gold watch and a proper easel when I passed my exams at the *Tech.*
Now I'm married to the boy next door, a decorator by trade!
He paints walls and I paint pictures, as we dream of plans we've made,
I still have dreams of Paris, my pictures on walls of a sidewalk café,
Dad my ever ardent fan says, 'Your dreams will come true, one day,'
I still paint *nice* pictures for him, words of wisdom he still imparts,
Reminiscing on my youthful zeal, I'd have cut off both my ears, for the
Sake of my blooming art.

J M Hefti-Whitney

POET

I am a poet
A rhymer of words,
I deal in nostalgia
Facts and absurds.
I dwell on the past
An incurable romantic
Anachronistic in view
With interests semantic.
No social message
Have I to impart,
The lines which I write
Come straight from the heart.
I write about nature,
About birds, about flowers
About rivers and mountains
Gardens and bowers.
Sun, sky and moon
Stars shining bright,
I write about day,
About dawn, about night.
Memories I describe
With inventive recall,
Or events in a childhood
Which never happened at all.
The words which I pen
You read out of choice,
For what are my poems
But my thoughts given voice.

John Bracken

COMPROMISE

Nobody loves a poet
A poetess rates even worse
The happily budding Shakespeare
Mustn't break out in verse
A verse is greeted in silence
The author viewed with pity
No use his being proud of
A thought out, respectable ditty
A limerick has to be funny
Then it may rate a smile
Condescension applied to the writer
Stands out the proverbial mile
A poetess is a phenomenon
Wasting her time with this rhyming
Be occupied better with housework
Or singing, or acting, or miming
Folk could then view what she's doing
To read it just isn't the same
A book now, a really good novel
She'd be on the right road to fame
A man, then, could emulate Dickens
That's something of which to be proud
For there really are very few poets
Who are standing well out from the crowd
Perhaps if they all made a promise
To neglect that proverbial moon
Their poems a mite more respected
If they ceased to rhyme Moon with June!

Doris Holland

SYMPHONY NUMBER SEVEN

Join Ludwig's manic, tipsy round-dance
Through the stars,
Or sing with bard Sibelius
Of life's ever-changing,
Theme-recurring ways.
Let song and dance, life-givers,
Abolish drear determinism's death and gloom.
May poetry, music, hail our rise
To rebirth and rebuilding,
Eternal cycle-big bang, big crunch.
'In my beginning is my end.'
In us the power lies
To tear apart dull present's blinding veil:
Seeing, hearing, tasting, touching, smelling
All that ever was
Or beyond far future's dark horizon
Lies as yet unborn.
'In my beginning is my end.'
E Major-radiant Bruckner's ode to joy,
As in the end the Heavens and the Earth
Create their God!

Alan Swift

MORE THAN ONE STRING TO THE BOW

Violins with their light *pizzicato*
Begin the tuneful conversation.
Viola's reply is mellow *legato*.

Cellos develop the theme *staccato*.
Husky double basses answer them
With comments that are molto *marcato*.

The melody made by hands and bow
Is stroked on the strings from high to low,
Finishing with flourish *sforzando!*

R E Ward

THE ARTIST WITHIN

Everyone is an artist, in their own special way,
We all can create in only a day,
The artist with paint, he captures the scene,
With colours on canvas, drawn to serene,
A song that is sung, so clear and so pure,
The model who struts on the catwalk demure,
Hands work with wood, sculptured so fine,
Architects drawing with such a fine line,
Designers create in their own special way,
Farmers in summer, their creation with hay,
Poets they write, paint a picture with words,
Politicians so cleverly make sure they are heard,
A child making models, they steadily grow,
Gardeners with earth all aligned with a hoe,
Writers of music, so sweet to our ears,
Stories and fables handed down through the years,
We all have an artist inside us to find,
There's an artist within, it's deep down inside.

W Curran

I WANTED TO KEEP YOU

I wanted to keep you,
To endlessly save.
Each eternal lost moment,
In a photo-frame cage.

I wanted to keep you,
Capture your warm animated face.
Drawn in soft pencil,
It is your silver image I trace.

I wanted to keep you,
Upon a gold locket and chain.
Open a clasp to a heart,
Engraved with your name.

I wanted to keep you,
Like some song in the mind,
So I composd a tune on a piano,
Wrote each note on a line.

I wanted to keep you,
Preserved in an evergreen age,
So I pressed you a flower
Upon a poem on a page.

I wanted to keep you.
I always wanted you to stay.
Now only your memory holds magic,
Like a sun setting on the edge of a day.

J A Lawrence

SIR JOHN

The tiny church of St Enodoc
Amongst the moving sands
In its little churchyard
So peacefully it stands.

In this quiet graveyard
There is a grassy mound
With a plain slate headstone
Herein a famous man is found.

Beside a long lost sailor
Shipwrecked upon the shore
And a brave young soldier
Killed in some forgotten war.

He was a mild and gentle man
Whose love of words and poetry
Made him the Poet Laureate
Sir John Betjeman.

Lydia E Stanton

TEARS RAINED DOWN

Once in a life-time in a bombed-out city
Came a great actor and he showed pity
The nights so dark, no street-lights glowing
People groped their way to hear him reciting.

'Shakespeare in Peace and War' was the title
It was an unforgetable recital
A curtained stage with its lectern of gold
Behind stood a man splendid to behold.

Silence intense as he started to read
A spot-light played but he did not heed
Sad, stirring, valiant were words he uttered
Unrestrained his tears, eyelids fluttered.

The Bard of old was still playing his part
A wonderful actor displaying his art
All could imagine the tragedies to come
Felt the call for courage to be passed on.
His vital presence filled that great hall
Fine his attire, he stood there so tall
The words were lyrical reaching so far
A wonderful experience, we found a star.

Hundreds of years and the Bard lives on
His knowledge of man will never be gone
A magical voice still rings in my ears
Will it circle the Earth for aeons of years?

Evelyn Sharman

NATURE'S ART GALLERY

Painted landscapes with shades of green,
Specks of multi-colour covering the land.
Magnificent trees unfolding their secrets of time;
Faces in the heavens becoming footprints in the museum.
Dancing flames growing and multiplying,
Creating a spectre of shapes.
Scents so enchanting,
Are carried in the wind.
Birds awakening life,
Waves slowing to the setting sun;
Create the music of life.

Ann-Marie Wall

I DON'T CARE WHAT PEOPLE SAY

Poetry.
My way
Of expressing myself,
As me
And no-one else.
I get angry when people laugh at my clothes,
But it's my grandmother's jacket,
Special to me.
I am expressing that
And I don't really care.
It's the same with my poems -
I don't care if people laugh,
Because it is what I want to do,
And at least people take notice
Of me
Being myself
If I was someone else,
People would laugh
Even more
I'm me
And I don't care what people say.

Fiona Stimpson

I WANT YOU TO FIND YOURSELF
(For the Gardzienice Theatre Association)

I want you to find yourself,
Stretch your frail, white hand
Into the blackened night
Just to see what it will draw forth.

Unclench the tightest jaw,
That of your mind,
Open its mouth and boldly drag
On whatever proffers itself
To those lips of yours,
For it too takes a risk.

Slip the latch,
Enter though you feel you have no right;
For what are rights if not restrictions,
Limits on an existance that should be limitless.

Find yourself
And watch the birthgiver
Of all your inhibitions
Reach longingly for a grave
Long overdue.

Dance,
Though it doesn't become you.
Walk in unshod feet,
Though the soil that bore you
Pricks.
Swim,
As life breaks her waters before you.

Your gestation is over,
Begin.

Ciaran Berry

MIDTOWN MOONDANCE

'Before my pen
Hath gleaned
My teeming brain'
I sit
Wonder ponder
Gathering information
Pouring down abundance
In torrential
Re-creation.

Before I write
The story
My gleanings remain
Sitting
Wondering pondering
Conjuring inspiration
Scoring 'Midtown Moondance'
In potential
Contemplation.

Now I recall
The memory
Of leaning remnants
Standing
Reminiscing remembering
Reviving inspiration
Exploring 'Mid-day Sundance'
In residential
Situation.

Alexander Shand Hudson

SUNFLOWER!

I once was a flower
That sat in the ground
When my petals fell
They did scatter around
The bees came to kiss me
The sun shone on my head
But nobody listened
To the things that I said
Then a man came along
With easel and paint
And now I'm so famous
That I hang in the Tate

Marie Nieuwoudt

LISA

Nothing excites me more,
Than the opera on channel four,
Stuck to my set like glue,
For the drama on channel two,
And when the dot departs,
It's goodnight to the arts,
Till another play,
On another day,
Stirs our wooden hearts,
To the gallery I often go,
To gaze upon the Mona Lisa,
Or the Venus de Milo,
Museums and Tutankhamen,
Hold my fascination,
As do antiques and relics,
And archaeological excavations,
Once I sit and read a book,
The world and its mother,
Could knock my door,
But they wouldn't
even rate a second look,
Who could fail to be impressed,
By the charm and passion,
Of the three tenors,
For them adulation
Is the current fashion,
An early night for me means,
My night nurse,
A paracetamol,
A brandy,
And the latest book of verse.

P J Littlefield

THE SWAN

Head erect: swan-neck held proud,
That daunting, unchanged expression.
She floats on seas of azure blue,
Her movement barely ripples the water.
With arched back she glides both straight and true,
Her grace carries her to her goal.
Slowly, her head tilts right then left,
As she drifts on that evening tide.
On her way she surveys those lesser souls,
This regal lady is aware of her true worth.
Although others may paddle and flap all around her,
Nothing phases this queen of the tide.
But, what is this? The azure seas are merely lights,
The ugly-ducklings are just parts that they play.
But for me this is my night of nights,
For me this is my rainbow's end.
Yet, this last night of 'Swan Lake': My poor heart breaks, how my
                              hands long to stroke and to preen her,
My life's course? *Love's first sight,* surely takes; yes, I'm in love
                              with the Prima Ballerina.

Bruce Ward

POETS ON POETRY

Why do I write?
I really don't know,
I get an idea,
And give it a go,
Across the page, my pen does fly,
Writing dwon things, I know not why,
I haven't a clue where I get my ideas from,
But I've got to jot them down quickly,
Before they are gone,
I write poems on a variety of subjects,
In different styles but always in rhyme,
As poems are boring and predictable if
When about the same thing all of the time,
Through my work I aim to amuse, to
Shock and scare,
To make people laugh or cry and some are
Written for a dare,
Some are messages I aim to get through,
But my main aim's to appear to everyone,
In every piece I do.

Emma Kemm

FIRST IMPRESSIONS

I can envy the art of 'Renoir'
Be enthralled by the skill of 'Degas'
find 'Manet' a treat,
'Claude Monet' exquiseet.
Though they pale at your beauty by far.

I admire all the shapes of 'Cezanne;
And those south island girls of 'Gauguin'
'Picasso' though new,
Was modernistic in blue,
Such virtue fires passion in man.

'Van Gogh' cut his ear off, they say
For love, like 'Lautrec' in his way
Who'd begged to stand tall,
Though their art said it all,
In you there is genius, I pray.

Michael Gardner

TRAVELLING IN IMAGINATION THROUGH ARTS

In music and verse you drift into places of beauty,
Far distant from the seeing eye;
Or re-live some days of tragedy
In which a dear one die.
Or go back in days of memory,
And see happiness and cheer as before.
You can travel almost anywhere,
Through imagination's door.

In drama too imagination travels far and wide;
Whether music, comedy or crime,
With grace the players glide.
With such posture, charm and dignity,
Your interest is rapt and intent,
In enjoyment you are held;
A happy evening spent!

Marjorie Cowan

AN EXTRACT FROM TORVILL AND DEAN THE EPIC 'BOLERO'

Prussian purple twisted within a strand of electric gold
Knelt; my legends, on an invisible carpet - wait
Alone, a single French horn, a harmony . . .
So very slowly each move to the military beat
Each movement commanded, arms outstretched horizontal, swaying
Drawing each other together, as if two magnets,
Ever so calmly you are placed on the ice
And circle around, impatient, so still you glide away
Into the fantasy that only you can fulfil; lead us -
Continuous you pull us along
As though each of us is attached to you
Longingly intensity of volume and oxygen rises
Tension builds, a tremendous extension of elevation
The masterpiece, restrictions blown away, the ultimate art-form
Your combinations of passion and sensuous seduction limitless
Transfixed
The haunting climax, ringing with death
To explain your story 'Bolero'
Clash of entangled instruments, the feeling of petrified panic;
No escape can be made, running away detrimental,
No-one can save the misery, the love so strong, too powerful,
Your plaintive cries will become a ghostly echo,
Distant and in the past.
Spinning, sweetly, spheres of speed too much
Two bodies colourless, lie, parallel on the frozen ice
Hands clasped still as in life, so still in death
Motionless
Even when static you still captivate
Roars of the most fantastic, frantic performance ever
Still haunts me now!

Linnet-Joy Allison

FIRST NIGHT

The scene is set, the stage is laid,
The audience, well, they all have paid
The toffees are being handed round
The papers thrown upon the ground
The stage is empty, so's my head
I wish that I had stayed in bed
Matilda Mary's lost her book
She's asking all the cast to look,
My heart is beating like a drum,
I wish that I had never come
Oh, holy smoke, here comes the vicar
Makes me feel just that bit sicker
Wonder, if, when in the pulpit he stands,
He ever gets sweat, coming out of his hands
But his audience of two, must seem a flea bite,
'Gainst what I see through the curtains tonight
Alright on the night, they keep telling me
But with that remark I fail to agree.

Dora Watkins

TWO LEFT FEET

To teach me to dance
When I could only prance
Was the job of Sarah Jane
Who lived down the lane.
Two left feet says she to me
With that I had to agree
She had patience no end
And she didn't pretend
That I was easy to steer
From there to here.
Your timing's so bad
She says it's just sad
But I have never failed yet
So I'll make you a bet
That waltz you will do
In one year or two.
I looked with a grin
And me just all in.
Thinking will my two feet
Then look so neat
When I waltz with great grace
And keep up the pace
Will Sarah Jane then say
'Let us call it a day'
A work of art to my name
I sure have achieved fame
I'll retire with a smile
And rest for a while.
Good-bye to my pupil
You're never more supple.

Brigid O'Donnell

RIVERDANCE

The dance is fluid
She flows over the land
Graceful river-woman
Shaking, waking hand

Summoned, compelled , commanded
By musical demand
Clouds and rain pervaded
Dry and barren land

As the earth awakens
Energy pulses, pounds
Sleep disperses slowly
Earth rises, new vitality found

Earth and river mingle
Timid, shy at first
Aware of coming glory
Miraculous, divine re-birth

Forces gain momentum
Unite in glorious dance
Tap out their exaltation
Love, joy, energy.
Stamp - stamp - stamp!

Elizabeth Loy

OH!

A streak of golden sunshine yellow
On rosy tints and heavenly blue
Torrents of turquoise so brash, yet mellow
Perfect brush strokes in every hue.
      But what is it . . . ?

I peer up close, then stand far back
Admiring bold lines and colour,
Oh! How I wish I could paint like that
In joyous, riotous splendour.
      What could it be . . . ?

If fills a wall, demands attention
'Just look at me,' it screams;
Splashes, waves in brilliant profusion
Tumble, clashing, as in dreams.
      I think maybe it's . . .

A storm tossed ocean filled with wrecks
Vermilion flashes - could be blood
Ochre crags split through with cracks
Or Noah's struggle through mighty flood!
      Or could it be . . .

Two spears of light from tortured eyes,
Or is it knives and two fried eggs?
And ketchup flung in twenty ways -
'Keep guessing,' gaudy canvas begs.
      It's coming . . .

Balls of flame with fiery spray
Cool pools of sapphire in eddies well,
Phantoms leaping, shadows play -
Ah! Here's a title - 'Peace in Hell' -
      Well, I'd never have guessed!

Mary Todd

A QUESTION OF ART

In the name of 'Arts Conception',
Reviews should match concern.
With language limiting concepts,
How can a layman learn?

A mixing of metaphors
Representation, and expression,
Has elevated materials
As the dominant impression.

We look into the sides of beasts,
Holes in wood and stone,
With influence of 'Expert Advice'
On quality, meaning and tone.

Is human skill and nature opposed
With these imaginative designs,
A concrete house, inside out,
What's the symbol? What's the sign?

Should we be sceptics,
Judgement suspended,
Doubt ingenuous artists
And the motives intended?

Is celebrity like undetectable gas,
Overcoming personal perception,
Shaping and stretching artistic taste,
And its loss of appreciative direction?

Ray Dite

WORDS

It's funny how most of the time,
My head is full of words and rhyme.
As I'm walking quietly down the street,
Contemplating what should I eat.
Words start chanting round my brain,
Repeating, repeating, again and again.
Often the words are strong and sad,
Analysing experiences that I've had.
Sometimes my mood is very light,
I see humour in everything in sight.
Privately I will start to laugh inside.
My hardest a smile I try to hide.
I have just thought up another ditty,
Rather funny and definitely witty.
Usually when I am tucked in bed,
Words stay for hours inside my head.
When I die the post mortem will surely find,
Many a verse in the recess of my mind.

Joan Vicente

ART AND JOY

What a joy one can find in art,
How my own daughter's life, did start,
Born was she, like others with a gift,
And now how her life . . . she does live.

Just taking a special pencil in her hand,
The gift of talent so young, we did not understand,
'God' knows who he wants things to make,
She's an illustrator, to London her work, her did'st take.

There are they, who act Hamlet,
How that story hast come to the front,
Art covers so much, we know,
Like painting the view, from the window.

The art of making a dress,
Knitting and making patterns too,
All of which could be designed by you,
Art and joy, give so much interest.

Like today, the computer and games,
With them life is never the same,
All add to less for folks to do . . .
What is your art . . . your joy?
Writing and singing maybe . . . all of which can make you happy.

Anita M Slattery

THE DESTINY

This is not a country for living souls
Recoiled the heart lives under the enshades
Of vampire ridden nature and all its parts
On beggarly sums amassed by the pauper
Of bleakness and cold, hunger and mort
Here existing we burrowing like moles
In drenched country termite eaten rocks.

There are no events, images happenings
But ever the same the generations waste
Cobwebbed on a bold spot their anger
In rimless cups in pale lipped liquors
Time eaten tales aimed at amusing
Lamenting on their irrecoverable loss
A loss which was never their gain.

Forward they go groping in search of substitutes
In hotel rooms where empty pouches hang
Over the pegs of wealth work and pleasure
All have accepted with hispid hands
Stiffening nature humbly no measure for measure.

It is not for the charter of world do we create
Burning our brains and light of our eyes
But each image in our mind creates
A correspondence image in the space
And each line of verse entombs
In eternity a sightless gong
Which the poet can hear with his subtle mind
In span of his wretched life and can find
Some solace when everything significant is betrayed
When the weed choked fields of this world can claim
Their foremost place on the altar of poesy.

Durlabh Singh

THE ARTS

He swaggers off down the road
Dressed in his football gear
Look at him, he's so bold
A hard case, never fear.
The arts? He hasn't got a clue
Although he *has* heard of Van Gogh
All artists are mad, that's true
In fact they must all be soft.
He doesn't realise art could be
Dance, music, drama, words
They paint in oils, you see
Portraits, landscapes, flowers, birds.
Don't talk to him about The Arts
As he kicks his ball against the fence
Not interested, for a start
Waste of money, waste of time - no sense.

Chris Ann Kent

WHAT DO 'THE ARTS' MEAN TO YOU?

Not a lot, if you ask me:
I like a bit of garden,
flowers, a tree - that's natural like -
but why they have to drown sheep
in some funny liquid,
or call red meat fetched off the hook
a living sculpture -
takes the biscuit.

Mind you, don't mind
a bit of jazz - boobidy boo boo -
on the quiet; but what a racket
when the kids go mad
on reggae, rock or
some such other fad,
piercing their ear-drums
with the beat so loud;
a bit of Rule Britannia's not so bad -
can't stand a crowd meself, though.

They say that watching telly
numbs the mind,
and anything that comes
is good enough for most -
can't boast I was the only one
to watch that Pride and Whatnot
- it were nation-wide -
and though I 'aven't read
the book, I might one day.
What did you say?
What do the arts mean to me?
Not a lot, really.

Maggie Goren

OUR DAMIEN AND OTHERS

What's this a cow in beer?
Dear me it's two I fear.
Damien is not the first
To have a terrible thirst.

Two chairs sat at the Tate
Were painted like a gate;
It's not my cup of tea
They're only there to see.

My! Found, something I like
An iron thing, like a bike.
No wheels but lots of steel,
And stays erect and noble,
Not down at heel.

It's in the RA court you know
Not far from Eros with his bow.
I saw a lot of art today
Bets to buy I will not lay.

John Spiby

UNTITLED

To have not
        And dream
Of having.
To put it into form
        And leave it.
For people in the arts
To say they are in the
Arts.

Joel Hammond

ANXIOUS SLOTH

'Where are you?'
Screamed the colours on the board.
'I thought you knew,'
I said, stepping back.

'Why am I here?'
Politely enquired the paper-support.
'What? - Oh - Yes -
You are here to prop up the colours
Whilst they try to find me.'

'Wait!' Wept the crayon
In my open hand,
'This isn't right, where do *I* go?'
'Well,' I sighed,
'I must rest,
And think
About that
One
Later.'

Mary Gill

FROM MY EXPERIENCE:

Expressing the inexpressible
- logic without the justification;
easy stabbing at the stars of conviction
with brush, pen or instrument:
scratching the blank surfaces,
striking the chords in echoes of vibration,
pigmenting a canvas,
moulding, carving, building, printing . . .

Daring to dig deep
to challenge the cliff face of mortality
plunging into the crevasse: where anger, sorrow and calamity
curse the Gods and their meddling -
resurfacing into smiles where
secrets unfold in endless variations
forming and reforming sounds of wonder,
illuminating pockets of resistance to
those graphic enterprises each era insists upon!

Yes, the arts mean:
        less of media, more of medium;
        transport without travelling;
        dancing in step with the psyche
        forever honest in reproducing
        effects affected by the maker
        whose creation can cause chaos
        hurling gems of promise
        into laps of lasting joy!

Wendy Sullivan

UNTITLED

Aboard the merry-go-round of more and better,
First and fast,
Perched with senses numb and feathers maimed,
Round and round,
We chase the hi-tech dream.

The axial blade scores deep with every turn,
A senseless crowing fills the air
Ribboned flesh
Hangs rank and sour,
A festered bunting in life's breeze.

Through time a glimmer comes and lights the anxious scene,
Shuffling feet advance to feel its warmth
Paper shells grasp the forgotten dream
Quick wingless flight,
Creation flushed, redeems this persistent canvas.

Pealed layers from a plastic doll
Sewn into the wind
Draw a vital trace
Life cluttered with empty phrases
Heavy with ornament
Only a dry pea in a bucket
Not known and in time to know no-one
Experience is all
And when competition fades into a clear blue sky
We are born anew.

Heather Muddiman

ARTFUL WAYS

Now, ask anyone, what is meant by 'The Arts',
and a different reply you will get -
the subject's so vast, and covers so much,
and depends on your life-style, and 'set'.
If by 'Art' you mean painting
then most likely you'll drool
before this old Master, or that.
Or, you might belong to the modern school,
your eyes glazing over, and rapt,
as they gaze and gaze at cubist art -
(perhaps getting confused, and wondering
just *where* did the artist *start?*)
But, you will never admit you don't know,
as you argue each 'pro' and each 'con'.
But, will the Old Masters be here
when the Cubists are finished - and gone?
There are other forms of art, of course,
and, just to take a few,
we mustn't forget drama and ballet,
and, again, it's the old and the new.
We were brought up on Shakespeare and Ibsen,
and all that modern theatre entails,
which means - today - horror of horrors -
the ballet, Swan Lake - with *males!*
So whether it's music, painting or sculpture,
or drama, or ballet, or both,
you really *must* do something 'Arty' -
otherwise you'll be labelled 'A Sloath'!

Joyce Hockley

IN THE GOOD ROOM
(For James 1934 - 62)

You admired the sketch that
leaned unframed against an old vase -
It was a good likeness then; fashioned
by an artist one 'fair-day' when
I was just seventeen.
We shared a desk at school,
and you were my brother's best friend;
still, perhaps we were seeing each other
for the first time. But over time
the profile was lost in the moving,
and I, in the standing still.

Mary Devlin

THE CANON OF ART

Difficult to say what it's about . . .
This thing called art,
There's so much of it for a start.
The eyes consume it greedily
The brain assimilates and cogitates
And shifts perceptions wearily.
Each raft of artefacts through the ages
Gives more information than any history book pages.
The moment of creation, execution and elation
Mirrors each era and artists' situation.

Today without rules to judge or acclaim,
No 'right' or 'wrong'; no 'this way up'
Or 'too short' or 'too long'
It is a work-it-out-for-yourself game.
What you see is what you get
So it's worth study time and intellect.
For us in our state of post-modern confusion
There is only one firm and sensible conclusion;
Think it through, make with care and tell what's true,
The canon of art is up to me and you.

Lyn Mowat

THE MASTERPIECE
At my feet,
Lie the broken fragments
Of the most wonderful piece of art
Ever made.

I made it.
I broke it.

Paul Frank Lewthwaite

MOTIVATION BLOCKAGE

Inertia, it come and it go with the force of a what?
Some ebb and flow it produce when sat on one's arse
Instead - mechanics of pointlessness pivots with
a whimper, impinges on fulcrum not one inch it does
Whilst you gaze at uneventful horizon reacting
To nothing as imagination fails to fire old synapse
Electrics short, and rusted buckets for bowels
Fail to move with freedom - inertia don't move
Or make way - trudge away from monomania man
Making himself up as he goes along - God knows
This hiatus between painting and impotence makes
Browsing through frightening and mordant reams
Of invisibility and aimlessness painful - see row
Upon row of neat scratched marked black blots
And caustic pigment broadcast in bold the lethargy
Of dead paint and canvas that segregate page from
Page with messianic arts skulduggery - he don't
Know what this all mean but he don't think
When scribbling he does.
He have major problem of movement - so fed up
With problematic posture of doing nothing but look
And wait - this proposition wants to make him lie
Procumbent - or go back to bed in prosaic lack of
Beauty - paint block spoils his rota routine but
Moved by presentiment of disaster to come but vague
As to its issue or what its expectation be
Give up altogether. He tried for a while
At least he tried - exhausted - good-bye.

Graham Hyde

ART IN NATURE
(From a photograph of an Andy Goldsworthy action sculpture)

The sculptor of the moment
flies a paperless unshaped kite,
intricate but disintegrating.
The camera, keener than the eye,
stabs this one flicker
when the bunched sticks
made, as they must, being just
their shape and size, and held just so,
and hurled
just so
at that place, on that day, in that wind, this
intersection of exact trajectories
intrinsic to them,
but needing this skilled innocent
to write with them on air
a word from the new testament.

Roy Blackman

THE CAROUSEL

'I've started, so I'll finish' I once joked - I have no option.
Aboard the carousel which will not stop, the music raucous
And the pace monotonous. Cymbals clash and drums begin to roll.
Poets prick dictators' dreams, and actors in a world of make-believe
Dislodge reality - whatever that might be - that old complacency.
Burn, cut, dig deeper into this hidden psyche, walk from room
To cavernous room, but do not lose the thread which guides you.
'The Arts' all separate yet intertwined, drawn from the deepest
Well of human feeling, flowing from the soul's ambition - their
                                                                  common source.
The city rises - and anchors big as houses, pulled by horses
From a Futurist Manifesto across the bridges of the Venice of the Midlands.
Round Oaks, Bilston Steel, a sky alight with furnace blasts,
A land which brooked no art, yet was itself a masterpiece of public art.
The eerie sound of lions at Dudley Zoo - hungry for their evening meal,
The forge's thunderous echo through the stillness of the night.
This was my childhood or so I think it now. Is it memory
Or imagination drawn from Blake or Dante's dark Inferno?
I know not, and I care not. I cannot make the separation.
For however high I climb, this landscape stretching far below
Is linked by unseen webs and chords umbilical to the very essence of my soul.
Its power, beyond the vagaries of fashion burns within my heart,
Roaring in the cauldron of my being, and deeper still the force
Of history beneath the surface of the memory, reveals the Sphinx and
                                                                     Aztec Temple.
Unseen and unknown craftsmen shipping stone by barge along the river
Make manifest the idols of a far off land, another century.
The bright side and the dark side of the moon - the left side and the
Right side of the brain - our equilibrium. Looking to the stars,
No vision without passion can accommodate the music of our senses,
The flight of swans above the lake.

Michael Lyons

SELF EXPRESSION

Strip free my body from its rags and its tatters,
Its jewels, its dresses, its gowns.
And let it be wild, let it be free,
Let spirits explode ecstatically,
No burden shall be bound.

For this is my essence, my core, my source,
My everlasting flame.
And my soul shall live and express itself
Like the sun through drizzling rain.

And then shall the source of creation
Be released into the air,
Be it love, joy or emotion,
Temper, rage or despair.

And when I am gone from this moment in time
The part that I shall leave behind,
Will be a vision of thought that once occurred
Deep within my mind.

E R Gemmell

MY ART

My art is my creation
of the lovely things I see,
With minimum exertion
I give a part of me.

Beauty is for the beholder
but as our talent grows,
And we become much bolder
and take in all the shows -

We see there's many different ways
of showing what we do,
How will we ever have the days
to give some part to you.

Josephine Miles

THE ARTS

an uncomfortable amalgam we are
of arrogance and a desperate eagerness to please

heart-stoppingly marketed -
a flyer from the soul to the wallet

dismissed as snobbery
labelled as luviedom
cotton-wooled on a higher plain
of cathedral-hushed tones and the reverence
of Radio 3 voices

there are special words for our places of workship:
gallery theatre concert hall studio cinema venue writing room

in them we strip down our beings, quake in the heat, ungod-like
Hephaistos, we forge presents for the world:
coded messages in welded steel and greasepaint, water-colour and
laser print, vibrating skins and strings and the shaking calves
of dancers

and when it's finally in the can we are allowed to grab
the falling handfuls of applause
stuff them in frantic to fill
the voids left by this repeated ECT
jolts of channelled synergy
euphoria a hit sharper and higher than smack
and still in its glow we unwrap our bleeding feet,
bandage our RSI, swarfega our fingers,
hit the town that's bleary with dawn
talking like there's no tomorrow
connections singing like arteries
looped fragile between us in thick blue
pulses as we swing out into the streets

and the world really has changed.

Char March

THE WORLD OF THE ARTS

Is it my job to co-operate in this process of confirmation
Daily rituals of placement
Proving self proving presence
Existence
Or is it my job to detach myself
Or not to attach myself
Not to confirm not to prove
Nor seek my presence
But to accept what happens
And react
Is this inquiring thought a reaction or a confirmation
Am I seeking answers or questions
Should we strive towards instinct or reason
Is one the antithesis of the other
Are they states of mind
Are we at best an amalgam of both
Is my awareness of everything around me a confirmation of myself
Or my purpose in confirmation of else
Is emotion regardless of conscience
A reaction
Instinct
Is conscience a reaction without reason
How much is all that we are psychologically a product of all that has been
Is reason a reaction
An instinct
Is instinct a reaction from existence from evolution
Is reason a progression or regression
Is our awareness of all else or anything else
In its totality
Our greatest fulfilment

Aodhan McCardle

THE ARTS CAN BE EVERYTHING

The Arts can be everything
Ends before starts
Means justified tarts
Bodies (whole and parts)
Seurat spot lights and darks
Cast but not made fast
Handmade paper darts
Franz Marc's animal arcs
Still bark in empty parks
Seminal larks with embalmed sharks
Flying past fart-filled flasks
(sponsored by Marks and Sparks)

There is even room for open hearts.

Andrew Tatham

QUESTIONS OF AUDIENCE, OWNERSHIP AND INTENTION

languid
slow bending of the notes
she sings to me
for this moment

audience is all
her genius
is to make me think
she sings for me

blue notes
white clefs and staves
the sky is his
for this moment

his painterly
appropriation
giving temporary
ownership

verbal notations
their pattern of feeling
caught in intention
for this moment

they are for you
all explorations
in the second
person singular

James M Nash

EXPRESSIONS OF PASSION

I know what poetry can do
It brings out the real you
Leaves nothing hiding away
Kept inside for the sake

Selfless is how it denotes
Holds no love in
It gets stroked
How much love it gives
When you write poetry
Happiness breathes

The expressions of passion it will never leave.

Anita Watts

IS THERE AN ART IN IT?

What is art can we agree
Some of it truly evades me
Twisted metal here and there
Three dimensional or a cubic affair
Picasso I never could understand
But Lowry to me is simply grand.
If it looks like a tree that's what it is
I don't want to have to gaze and quiz

Is it a bird or is it a plane
I can't be bothered having to guess
My head is aching taxing my brain
It's just another artistic mess
Constable had the right idea
So did Gainsborough things were very clear
A mountain's a mountain the sea's a sea
And in my mind that's how it should be

Not knowing if a picture's upside down
Is taking things too far I'd say
Abstract art is beyond my taste
It inspires me not - it's such a waste
But Lowry with his Matchstick Men
Portrays Northern life again and again.

Anthony Gibson

PAINTING A CREATION

Canvas, lies like a blank white page,
paint! It cries as though in a rage.
Not quite so simple, you might say,
as you keep the anger at bay.

Amid the chaos, of thought; one interprets the vision,
disregarding any thoughts of a mission.
Putting charcoal to canvas, dissolves the anguish,
like water on fire, now to extinguish.

Concentration, comes into play
disregarding what others might say.
Giving vent to true expression,
is the object of the lesson.

Open-mindedness, required inner-strength,
to go on at great length.
Then comes the sense of achievement;
on other's faces believement.

Realising, a creation,
is simply better, than any elation.

Alastair Buchanan

ACTING

To act is to be someone that you're not.
Forget for a few hours the problems faced
And take upon oneself another's lot.
To live it to the full with style and grace.

To feel that person's suffering - weep their tears,
Love with their love and laugh through all their joys.
Share with them all their hopes and all their fears,
Shout with their anger when something annoys.

Yet to each part I give a part of me.
The hidden parts that I dare not express.
Sometimes the person that I'd like to be,
Sometimes the darker side that I repress.

E Smith

A LANDSCAPE OF WATER COLOUR, PASTELS AND 2HB

Brushstrokes with motion and movement
landscapes with oceans of sky
smoking billowing puffing clouds
pillow-soft to rest when I lie

Pastel trees with shady boughs
knotted bark in 2HB
yellow flowers at searching root
blades of smudged grass in whispering breeze.

Pools of blue from swirling brush
the dipped wet hair of badger bristle
rest between the proud crowned head
of drying swaying purple thistle

Searching glints of golden sunlight
catch birds in soaring animation
their silent songs lost in the canvas
heard only in the voice of imagination

In the distance walking couples
playful dogs with sticks to bring
and in the foreground the artist's name
who lets us decide what his painting means.

James S Jarvis

SPECIALLY COMMISSIONED

From a dragon tearing through a chest,
To a peacock resting on a breast.
You could have an alien climbing your thigh,
Or on your shoulder an unblinking eye.
Your idols engraved into your skin,
Make your choice and we can begin.

With a stencil to follow I lay down my frame,
Carefully laying lines my needles to use again.
The outline complete and the skin wiped clean,
In my mind's eye the finished piece can be seen.
Now to bring it to life with shade and colour,
Using light and dark to compliment each other.

Commissioned by people to decorate their skin,
Sensing their anticipation as we prepare to begin.
Permanent markings records of things in life,
Reflections of good times and sometimes strife.
The choices are endless too many to mention,
Making your choice carefully should be your intention.

Some time spent under the tattoo gun,
Your choice has been made the design is done.
Finished now though he'll see you again,
As soon as your mind has forgotten the pain.
Already planning to fill another space,
It won't be long 'til you're back in this place.

Paddy Douglas

TRIBUTE TO PAM AYRES

I'd like to thank a lady
Who's given so much pleasure;
Her rhymes and verses through the years
Are those I'll always treasure.

She has the talent and the wit
To bring to all a smile;
And her delightful accent
Makes listening worthwhile.

So, I say, if you need a lift
Out of your daily cares,
I cannot better recommend
The lady named Pam Ayres.

Geoff Tullett

MONET'S GIFT

The brushstrokes of perfection
carry the message of beauty across the centuries.
The viewer intrudes upon that cherished moment,
when summer sun bathed the tranquil scene
in a shaft of golden glory.
Trees at attention, salute the glorious day
and carry the mind's eye
to the promised borders of this luscious landscape.
Ladies - the mothers and daughters of history -
parasols in hand,
hiding form the harsh heat of the day,
make their way, through the bejewelled patchwork pastureland,
silently stepping,
amongst the glowing sapphires, emeralds and rubies
carpeting their precious walkway.
Footsteps illuminated by the scented flowers
that welcome their tread.
At this moment, all is one,
Painter and paint celebrating the gifts of nature,
while the white-robed silhouettes enjoy the companionship
of this shared day.

Bettina Jones

ART FORM

I've always respected the art of words
Words can bring pain or pleasure
Words can be turned into something unique
A great art form to treasure

Often taken for granted
Something we use everyday
A poet can put them in order
And make them sound OK

Artistically looking so simple
We could have done it ourselves
It would have been easy to write it
But it was written by someone else.

Fred Tighe

THE PICTURE

The pictures were lovely. We enjoyed our job.
To catalogue them was a treat.
They varied from snow scenes to pictures of trees
In summer - some were quite a feat.

There were many gouaches and oil paintings too.
The artists showed design and skill.
Though amateurs, they loved the field of their choice
And painted landscapes with a will.

First 'Winter in Lapland' we wrote on our list.
Oh, this was a beautiful sight.
Then 'Autumn, Snowdonia' we added next
And hung it to catch the best light.

We came to a picture and then held it up
To distinguish bottom from top.
We turned it about and we could not decide.
This time we were caught on the hop.

'I think it goes this way,' my colleague said then.
'This looks like an old dry stone wall.'
'I think that it's this way,' I said, turning it,
'This abstract's the worst of them all.'

'Let's look for a title,' I said hopefully
'It may shed some light on the scene.'
We turned the print over and saw on the back
'This picture's called *Friday Night's Dream*.'

But even with problems the pleasure was ours.
It's a privilege to work with art,
To see splendid paintings gave us such great joy
That with our jobs we'd never part.

Joyce M Turner

CORNELIUS CRUD

Cornelius Crud, the younger sat in contemplative thought
'I ought to write a song,' he said
'Or read a book
Or learn to cook
Or take me for a walk'
But he sat upon the sofa staring at the window pane
And noticed that the day had turned to rain
Yet he had a sort of notion
That if he could get in motion
Then the sun might very well come out again

It was six feet to the window
It was ten feet to the door
But Cornelius's feet
Remained firmly on the floor
By the sofa where he sat
Till his head began to ache
And his hands began to shake
Just from thinking of the effort
That his bones would have to make

So he sank into the sofa
And closed his weary eyes
While the song remained unwritten
The book remained unread
The walk was never taken
And nobody was fed
For Cornelius Crud, the younger was effectually dead.

Brenda Soderberg

A POET

Poets have a way with words
Express feelings not always heard.
Voice opinions, have a say
Written words in a special way.
Poets can travel far and wide
In their thoughts and minds inside
Can go up the highest mountains
Swim in the deepest seas,
Poets have the world at their feet
People from everywhere to greet
Places to travel far away
Written in words, a special way.

Sheila Waller

MUSIC LESSONS

The resident professor of kazoo symphonia,
Came to our music class.
He asked me frankly about my failings,
And which theories I couldn't grasp.
Well simply old chap,
As I patted his back,
Our teacher will have to go.
As we music lovers,
have not even covered,
Whether we suck or blow.

John Kelly

OPENING NIGHT

The scene is set rehearsals done and costumes made
For everyone.
Long months of toil, sweat and tears now at last
Opening night appears.
From dressing room a nervous chatter, oops falling props
what a clatter.
A head appears around the door and shushes everyone once more.
Layers of gunge on faces slap, which shade is best,
This or that and ladies wishing they were not so fat.
Last minute panic a nervous cough, frantic search for cotton
As bits drop off.
Sharing, lending, primping and patting, pinning and tying,
All finger and thumbs it's all so trying.

'On stage'
'On stage'

The call goes out, the orchestra's going full pelt. A rustle
Of skirts a clanking of chains, there's enough metal round
Necks to addle the brains.
Shuffle in wings all hot and crowded, with shawls and wigs
Around faces shrouded.
Already the greasepaint begins to glisten, whilst straining for
The cues the chorus listen.
Here we go fingers crossed, toothy smiles mid-glorious locks
Hope to God it goes alright -
Still after all it is only opening night.

C Clarke

MODERN ART

I stand beside the Mayflower
a beautifully painted ship
and wonder what it would have been like
if I'd have painted it.

The Mona Lisa glares down at me:
those bewitching eyes have me hooked
calmly I smile back at her -
and she gives me a withering look.

I engage in gazing at Constable
(truly countryside art)
the Haywain I recognise from many a home -
the epitome of horse and cart.

But then I live in the modern world
not the art gallery of my mind
the world of concrete and stone and brick:
art of the starkest kind.

However, it is said that walls have ears
(they certainly have graffiti)
So is an art gallery a work of art itself?
It is, but it's not so pretty.

Julie Ashpool

ESSENTIAL DRAMA

If I chose at this point to have three boys dancing
Enter stage left like leopards prancing
And a girl in shock throw a central fit
While the drums run wild in a house ill-lit,
Would all stand on their seats shouting, 'This is it!
The greatest drama of the age!

Better litter the stage with fifteen dead
Dying methodically, foot on head,
As the blood runs down with sluggish care,
Then slip from the theatre soon as I dare -
My exiled feet on the pavements bare
The greatest drama of the age.

But heroines crowned with terrible hair
Pass in the street, oh turn and stare!
Five tragic acts are not so great
As a man in the crowd arrives too late
For the waving hand, the closing gate -
The greatest drama of the age.

Alasdair Aston

INFORMATION

We hope you have enjoyed reading this book - and that you will continue to enjoy it in the coming years.

If you like reading and writing poetry drop us a line, or give us a call, and we'll send you a free information pack.

Write to

        Arrival Press Information
        1-2 Wainman Road
        Woodston
        Peterborough
        PE2 7BU